Rediscovering Christian Realism

Rediscovering Christian Realism

A Common-Sense Approach to Contemporary Christian Living

JAMES E. HASSELL

RESOURCE *Publications* • Eugene, Oregon

REDISCOVERING CHRISTIAN REALISM
A Common-Sense Approach to Contemporary Christian Living

Resource Publications
An Imprint of Wipf and Stock Publishers
199 W. 8th Ave., Suite 3
Eugene, OR 97401

www.wipfandstock.com

PAPERBACK ISBN: 978-1-6667-5514-5
HARDCOVER ISBN: 978-1-6667-5515-2
EBOOK ISBN: 978-1-6667-5516-9

09/12/22

For those who commit to the impossible possibilities of life

Contents

Acknowledgments

Sincere appreciation goes to editors and publishers with Wipf and Stock for taking a risk on a rather unsexy topic. Discussions about Christian Realism may never "move the needle" on book sales, but its relevance abides.

The seeds of this book were sown about twenty years ago in numerous seminary classes regarding Christian Ethics. Giving adulation to the professors at both Logsdon Seminary and George Truett Seminary is not enough, considering how they prompted a thirst for lifelong learning and pursuit of the truth. Nonetheless, I rejoice in every remembrance of you.

Introduction

Christian Realism is one of the most viable solutions for people who struggle to overcome today's divisive culture. Christian Realism is defined here as the rejection of both idealism and nihilism in favor of a more biblical, common-sense perspective for an individual's participation in everyday relationships. We can be free from having to choose between the two most promoted sides of contemporary Western society—religious legalism and humanistic liberalism. We may rather seek to live in a better tension between healthy individuality and strong community.

Christian Realists accordingly pray for God's Kingdom to come on earth as it is in heaven. Yet they also look for the most appropriate solutions to complex and even unsolvable dilemmas. There are times when the command to love God and love neighbor becomes nearly untenable. What do we do in those situations? We find that only the empowerment of the Holy Spirit can help us live in a tension between what is and what ought to be. God is accordingly viewed as the primary Character, or what H. Richard Niebuhr called the ultimate "Value Center" around which our lives revolve.[1] Popular political ideologies—either conservative or liberal—become less central and less tied to Christianity in this more realistic way of thinking, praying, and ultimately living.

---

1. Niebuhr, *Radical Monotheism and Western Culture*, 116–18.

Introduction

The main idea of this book may be stated thusly: Christian Realism helps fallible but evangelistically determined Christians on their journey to walk just like Jesus walked. We will thereby aim to make some of the particulars of Christian Realism, especially as espoused by Reinhold Niebuhr, H. Richard Niebuhr, Emil Brunner, Paul Tillich, and John C. Bennett more accessible and palatable to a wider audience in order that we may imitate and follow Christ with greater effectiveness. We are ultimately aiming to describe and enact consecrated common sense.

But what is realism, really?

A discussion of Christian Realism begins with some observations about reality, in and of itself. We offer in this volume that reality may be defined simply as what is.

Put theologically, we are talking about ontological realism, or the recognition of that which exists apart from how we feel about it. James V. Schall captures the essence of such realism: "Reality is not something of our own making but is a gift given to us."[2] Christian Realism accordingly asserts that such a gift must come from a benevolent Giver and Creator. The created cannot become the Creator. The created must then accept reality as it is from a Source outside of ourselves.

But how do we know true reality? Human beings are obviously fallible, so attempts to concretize truth seem quite arrogant. Only objects can truly be objective. Yet, we do have the capacity to recognize two primary qualities to a given object. One is essence (the "whatness" of something) and the other is existence (the "thatness" of something).[3] Take, for instance, Timothy Mosteller's simple yet quite coherent illustration of a crow and a fence. Let's say that we look outside and see a crow sitting on a fence. Through mere observation, we surmise that both the crow and the fence exist. They have "thatness." Yet, they are different in essence. A crow has crow-ness and a fence has fence-ness. Reality, therefore, is what is.

2. Mosteller, *Heresy of Heresies*, 16.
3. Mosteller, *Heresy of Heresies*, 24–31.

It is not arrogant to say that the crow and the fence are not figments of our imaginations, nor are they mere categories of knowledge that we somehow create and project on to objects that we have been culturally conditioned to call a crow or a fence. A crow is a crow. A fence is a fence. Reality is what is.

But why can't we change crows into fences? Anything should be possible if you set your mind to it, right? Not really. The contemporary fascination with discarding reality as a myth has its roots in what is typically called modernity. We can trace modernity back to at least the late 1200s when philosophers such as William of Ockham proposed that essences are simply culturally conditioned names. In other words, a crow has "crow-ness" because that's the label we put on crows. So, if we removed the label, then we could possibly find that the crow's identity and existence were much broader and dynamic than what we observed in the daily life of crows.[4] We would then be free to turn a crow into a fence.

Such thought came to maturity in the philosophies of Rene Descartes and Immanuel Kant. Descartes doubted both the essence and existence of objects in the observable world. In fact, the closest Descartes ever came to certainty was his observation that he was a thinking being ("I think, therefore I am."). He could not even count on his own body being real. All he could settle on was the fact that he was having thoughts, and thus he surmised that he had some form of existence, whatever that may be.[5]

Kant seemed to pick up where Descartes left off. He offered that reality cannot be fully known, although we experience what we think is reality through filters, or categories. These categories were said to be conditioned through language, culture, and social forces. Kant, either knowingly or unknowingly, opened the door to relativism.

If any of this sounds familiar, it is due to American culture's firm entrenchment in Kantian philosophy. In fact, Americans today may believe more in relativism than in reality. Our culture has essentially glommed onto the Kantian teaching that reality is just

4. Mosteller, *Heresy of Heresies*, 87.
5. Mosteller, *Heresy of Heresies*, 88–89.

what we make of it. After bathing Kant's philosophy in the politics of Descartes, we have gotten to a point of making reality relative to the categories of our understanding. We consequently say things like, "This is my truth, and that's your truth." In other words, it's like saying, "If you want a crow to be a fence, then that's fine. Who am I to argue? The crow is just called a crow because of my background and heritage."

The most apparent Achilles Heel of relativism however is its litmus test of how true something can or cannot be. To make an absolute statement such as, "There is no such thing as absolute truth" is a logical fallacy. Little does the relativist realize that, regardless of our language and culture, a crow is still a crow regardless of the word we use for it. We can know reality in spite our philosophical categories and language because truth is truth.[6]

Christian Realism may therefore be called consecrated common sense. It is the recognition of reality by Jesus' followers, the disavowing of watered-down and unbiblical treatment of God and neighbors. Christian Realism does not insist on bringing about some idealistic nirvana on earth, but it also rejects the nihilism of thinking that the world has totally gone to hell in a handbasket. It is also concerned with what is, not with trying to make crows into fences.

Yet, Christian Realism is unafraid of testing truth claims. It will not shy away from disagreements about crows and fences. Christian Realism is no blind faith. In fact, this kind of realism weds reason and faith. John C. Bennett puts it thusly: "Christian realism is the avoidance of the illusions of both the optimists and the pessimists."[7]

The cloudiness of illusions to which Bennett refers can give way to the bright skies of reality due to our faith in Jesus Christ. We can be free to ask pertinent questions like: How can we test truth in light of the biblical narrative and our experience? What are ways that our pretensions can be tempered and humbled? How can we be optimistic about life without giving in to sentimentalism? What is the responsibility of both the individual and the community?

---

6. Mosteller, *Heresy of Heresies*, 93–109.

7. Bennett, *Christian Realism*, xx.

Ultimately the answers to such questions are found in focusing on the life, teachings, death, and resurrection of Jesus Christ. The Lord is both the starting point and the finish line of Christian Realism. But we must ask how we can begin to explore, understand, and embrace Christian Realism, especially if it is a foreign concept to us.

"He Went About Doing Good" (Acts 10:38)

We begin an exploration of Christian Realism by examining that which is popularly known as the common good. Many, if not most, Americans may view their contribution to the common good as essential to a meaningful life. But what is the common good? American society seems to understand the common good as that which is the most equitable response to human conflicts. Popular political and religious leaders may even promise an ideal, heaven-on- earth existence if we elect them to accomplish their ideas of the common good. Christian Realism however suggests that such an idealistic view of progress unwisely opens the door for too much power to be put in the hands of too few. We want to deal with what is.

Could it be then that we humans are our own worst problem?[8] In other words, before we talk about finding the common good, perhaps we should put more of a spotlight on our sinfulness than on either social or historical causes to our problems. When we merely blame social constructs for society's ills, we fail to take ownership of our own sin. We may even be prompted to violent action towards others because it is somehow beneath us to focus on our sin and finitude. The anxiety of our individual and corporate sin can lead us to implement all sorts of unsavory tactics to define and enforce our version of the common good.

Christian Realism helps us shine a bright light on our own mess-ups to deal with such anxiety. In fact, only a more complete trust in God will provide the relief for which we desperately search.[9] Power in the hands of the few, even if those few have relatively good

8. Niebuhr, *Nature and Destiny of Man*, 1.
9. Niebuhr, *Nature and Destiny of Man*, 3.

intentions, is subject to highly corrosive self-interests and must be held in check. We should accordingly ask if there is another way to find and do the common good by taking reality into consideration rather than simply going along with how the common good is defined by a powerful or popular group who are ultimately anxious concerning their relativized ways and means.

The Bible appears to give a much different definition of the common good than the one promoted in contemporary pop culture. We learn that Jesus "went about doing good," which specifically refers to ways Jesus treated others every day. Consider, for instance, that Jesus had little to say about politics. He took few ques, if any, from the Roman government to bring in his kingdom. You would probably not find Jesus at a Roman leadership conference. Also, our Lord showed little concern with his own popularity. He subsequently never coerced certain groups for his advantage nor held economic power over anyone. Yet, Jesus still managed to do absolutely what is right and good for others. He held in perfect tension the temporal and eternal in a perfect, realistic balance. His scales never tipped towards some mystical ideal or stunted cynicism.

Jesus' behavior and example suggests that the common good should be left neither to an individual in our society to define nor to the popular group in power in a given society. The reframing of our attitude towards ourselves and others in the way of Christ is thus the foundation of Christian Realism. Such realism implores us to define what is right and good not by how any world system, popular group, guru, or religious leader try to define it for us, since we are too plagued by finitude and self-interest. Rather, we find and ultimately do what is right and good by mimicking Jesus Christ in the fullest sense possible for us. We also keep in mind that the pride of life consistently gets in our way since we are sinful beings. The ultimate litmus test for what is true and good is Jesus. Yet, our idealism about doing the right, Christlike thing must be tempered by both our capacity to do wrong and our acknowledgment of God's grace. Christians are not Jesus, but we do have his Spirit living in us.

The question should not be, "What is the common good," but rather, "How do I behave like Jesus, considering my flaws and the complexities of life, to do the most good in view of God and my neighbor?" As we answer this question, we will not have to talk ourselves into doing something we call good based on being liked or getting power over others. Emil Brunner says it like this: "The good is not based upon a principle but upon a process of divine restoration, through justification by grace through faith alone."[10] In other words, you'll be able to do what is right and good because of the reality of God's grace and forgiveness of your sin and not because of your so-called superior intelligence or affiliation with a group which is on the so-called right side of history. We need consecrated common sense which only comes from the God Who Is—the One who defines what is.

But how? Radical Monotheism

If good flows from a process of divine restoration, then obedience to God and God alone leads to our doing good. To become good is to recognize and repent of sins and believe in Jesus Christ. True goodness starts when life doesn't revolve around us, our group, or the reality which is dictated by the majority in power. It does start however when our ultimate center of value is Christ Jesus.

When people become reverently serious in making the Person of Christ the ultimate value center, then they are well on the way to embracing and applying the reality of what is both individuality and in a community of people with consecrated common sense. In fact, there is a specific name for the reorientation process of putting Christ at the center called "radical monotheism," a term coined by H. Richard Niebuhr.[11] Radical monotheism is a biblical pathway for enacting Christian Realism and therefore walking as Jesus walked. Let's define the term and explain it with some depth.

Radical describes that which is beyond the norm. Monotheism refers to the worship of one God only. There is to be no room for any other gods in our life. Consequently, radical monotheism means that we are to go above and beyond any other subject of loyalty and allegiance in our lives to serve God only in relation to

10. Brunner, *Divine Imperative*, 67.
11. Niebuhr, *Radical Monotheism*, 31–37.

what is. Radical monotheism embraces God's grace and forgiveness of our sins, and it rejects loyalty to idols, or things that we put in the place of God. It helps us to recognize that we are fallen, sinful people, and there is accordingly no room for pretense. There but by the grace of God we go. Failure to commit to radical monotheism can lead to tremendous heartache, most often characterized either by idealistic fanaticism or cynical withdrawal.

Where are we headed?

This volume is written in a logical progression so you can understand how radical monotheism reorients the entirety of your everyday living around true reality of the way, truth, and life of Jesus Christ. Accordingly, we will explore a Bible-based reorientation process through which one can become more radically monotheistic and therefore realistic. We specifically will discuss the need for radical monotheism today and how it is applied through something called "confessional theology," based on biblical teachings and guidance from the Holy Spirit.

1

Reorientation to Christian Realism through Radical Monotheism

Radical monotheism functions as a powerful engine for the Christian. Its combustion propels a believer away from the traps of both pretentious idealism and cynical skepticism and towards embracing reality. How does it work? Radical monotheism reorients believers to keep themselves from being swayed by either legalism or relativism—those ideologies that typify the most popular, yet non-realistic forces among contemporary Christians in the West today. To embrace radical monotheism is to reject the polar ideological ends of non-realistic thinking in favor of a more balanced, realistically tested faith in Christ.

For clarity, it may be helpful to give some further definition to both legalism and relativism and their harmful effects on the Christian experience. Legalism is defined here as the philosophy which drives people to enforce rules and regulations to such an extreme that they hurt or even abuse others. Legalism is a mechanism by which people force their beliefs on everyone else. It operates from a strictly black and white, or "either/or" perspective. If someone is judged to be in the wrong, then he/she must face correction or be ostracized. There is consequently little wiggle room to account for historical context and human frailty in decision making. Christian legalists tend to promote their version of truth to the point of becoming violent or at least seeking to impose truth through nationalistic legislation, or by combining government and religion.

Relativism is almost the opposite of legalism and serves as a reactionary force against the conservative tendencies of legalists. It refers to the rejection of most rules since most, if not all truth, is relative. It asserts that what is truth for me may not be truth for you. Relativists subsequently care little about what is right and wrong unless another is doing activities that negatively affects them. For relativists, Christianity is primarily a private, passive affair and should be kept that way.

Radical monotheism reorients both legalists and relativists to a more realistic perspective by shining a brighter spotlight on Jesus. Consider Christ's example. He was neither a legalist nor a relativist. He was not a stickler about many of the religious rules of his day, especially the man-made ones. He healed others on the Sabbath day, ate and hung out with unpopular people, and simply loved people who were not regarded in his time as loveable. Yet, Jesus always did what was right, good, and truthful. Jesus not only believed in absolute truth, but he claimed to be the actual embodiment and personification of truth itself. We could say that Jesus Christ is the ultimate Reality.

It's not that Jesus rejected religious rules, but he both fulfilled religious rules and put the rules into their proper place. Based on his example, we may assert that should a rule fail to help us love God or love each other better, then it's not a good, realistic rule. Everything in a religiously legal sense must hang on the love of God and neighbor. So, yes, we must follow some rules to keep us loving God and loving each other in better ways. But to be a radical monotheist means that we follow the right rules in the right way—with love of God and neighbor always coming first. We also can assert that some rules will not be helpful and realistic in complicated, complex situations that require us to do the best we can with the most truth we have in view of our finite human nature.

Getting Some Context

But how does one become reoriented from either legalism or relativism to radical monotheism? Some background on the modern-day, polarized American religious situation will greatly help our understanding. It is however important to note that the following explanation can in no way be construed as exhaustive. Perhaps the following description, based mainly on the writings of H. Richard Niebuhr, will illustrate how today's American Christians have become increasingly unrealistic and decreasingly aware of biblical truth.

We could argue that American Protestant Christians today seem to have only two choices for living out their faith in a productive manner. They can either be conservative/fundamentalist or humanistic/liberal. The conservative way of thinking and living comes out of legalism, while the liberal way comes from relativism. It is important to note that we didn't get to this polarized environment overnight. In fact, the concepts of modern-day religious conservatives and liberals are rooted deeply in both American history and our societal DNA.

H. Richard Niebuhr's succinct chronicling of historical American theologizing becomes quite beneficial at this point. His research indicates that, as a result of the Protestant Reformation and the Renaissance, many Christians in the New World took what is called a "higher view" of God, and they especially resonated with biblical teachings on God's sovereignty. These Christians subsequently grew skeptical of human monarchies to the point at which many were rejected in favor of God's Kingship. The idea of the priesthood of all believers took root, especially in the 16th-18th Centuries, and a tremendous shift in church leadership arose in which laity took a much more active role in discerning the will of God for their local congregations. This heavy emphasis on giving political and religious power back to the people in a more democratic way seemed to contribute greatly to the establishment of the United States. It also eventually resulted in a relatively healthy plurality of religious organizations around the nation of all different theological and organizational stripes.[1]

1. Niebuhr, *The Kingdom*, 51–87.

Yet, the Reformation and Enlightenment also sowed the seeds of what is now the chaotic polarization among Christians in the United States. Protestant Separatists emerged during the Great Awakening, and they formed two main camps of Christian expression. One camp of Separatists embraced an extreme form of religious legalism and desired to ensure that their congregational and political bodies maintained a certain level of purity in service of God the King. The other camp reacted against legalism in favor of a kind of mysticism which desired to forgo much in the way of legal constraints to allow optimal emotional and spiritual fervor.[2]

By the 1730s, particularly with the dynamic leadership of pastors and theologians such as Jonathan Edwards, the more evangelical Protestants sensed a desire to hasten the culmination of God's Kingdom. The seeds of the "American Dream" and "Manifest Destiny" started here under the insinuation that America was a New Israel, a Promised Land that would finally be under the full direction of God, the westward movement of which was of particular interest, much to the demise of Native Americans. One may even offer here that nationalistic Christian thinking, mixed with an ardent form of racism, impacted not only American western expansion and the subsequent slaughter of Native Americans but also became justification for numerous later wars. Nationalism and racism are indeed a toxic cocktail, the poisonous effects still of which are felt almost daily in the contemporary political turmoil of the nation.

Others who were more hesitant to hop on the manifest destiny bandwagon, pushed back against the legalistic brand of Christian life by embracing a form of humanism in the nineteenth century and early twentieth centuries, resulting in what eventually became the social gospel movement. They paid particular attention to the poor and disaffected workers of the Industrial Revolution. Farther to the South, the legalistic tenants of the Great Awakening solidified in ways that went beyond nationalism. It became increasingly difficult to think of Christianity in terms of social action, so much so that many churches essentially went on the defensive, attempting to institutionalize the emotional quality and the conversionist

2. Niebuhr, *The Kingdom*, 91–119.

preaching of the Awakening. What resulted was the idea, especially promulgated in the South, that American Christians are a chosen people set upon conquest for the Kingdom, and they must protect the codified doctrines of the Great Awakening at all costs—even if such means making and keeping significant gains in the arena of federal government.

The humanists of the North and the legalists of the South naturally formed two intensely different forms of doctrinal, theological, and ecclesial action. The legalistic form, called "revivalism," is primarily that which gave birth to what we know in the present day as Christian conservatives, or fundamentalists. Revivalists key in still on some of the basic premises of the first Great Awakening, some of which include large meetings calling for conversion, emotional worship that can border on mass manipulation, and the connecting of the Kingdom of God to a Christianized American society. Revivalists, while valuing some forms of social action, remain hesitant and somewhat skeptical of any good work that does not quite fit into a conversionist dynamic.

The relativistic form is now called Christian liberalism, or progressivism. This form remains reactionary against conservatism, meaning that even many liberal Christians question the validity of a stanchly "right and wrong" axioms of truth. Liberal people would be less rules oriented than conservatives on many issues. One quite positive thing about liberalism is its focus on doing good deeds for others, at least through voicing of intentions to do good. Sometimes conservatism's rules can lead people to miss opportunities to do good. Yet, some more liberal Christians often participate in something called "group think." Group think happens when individuals place too much value on whatever is the most popular ideas of their friends or political party. Intentions seem to take precedence over real, hands-in-the-dirt actions or results.[3]

In other words, someone in a liberal group may have differing opinions on certain issues from the group, but the person discounts his or her own opinion to be accepted into the group and not be kicked out, especially if that person's intentions seem "bad" to the

3. Niebuhr, *The Kingdom*, 127–98.

group. Some may even believe that there is something wrong with them or that they are less valuable than others because they don't think and act just like everyone else.

The importance of good deeds for liberals also seems to be measured in terms of cultural relevance and popularity. Some of the more popular liberal good works today may include things like making sure that the government takes care of everybody. They will likely promote political ideals such as universal health care, democratic socialism, declaring amnesty for illegal immigrants, overhauling or defunding law enforcement, and battling perceived and real greed in leaders of the most well-known American businesses.

Needless to say, a sharp divide between many conservatives and liberals remains today in America. Radical monotheism does not attempt to repair this divide through further polarization. The point is not to argue with people as to the merits of conservatism or liberalism over the other. The point is to provide another way of living and thinking that plants its roots in reality—namely the revelation of Jesus Christ and the unconditional grace of God made possible in the atoning death and resurrection of Christ. Christian Realism is not an "either/or." It is a "both/and."

But how are legalism and relativism out of touch with reality? H. Richard Niebuhr perhaps best defines Christian liberalism as "a one-sided view of progress" in which "a God without wrath brought men without sin into a Kingdom without judgment through the ministration of a Christ without a cross."[4] Liberalism's doctrine seems too subjective, meaning that the truth of Jesus and God's Word is often held too loosely, depending on which way the cultural winds are blowing. Put succinctly, Christian liberalism misses the reality of human self-interest. It forgets that those who devote themselves to the common good, although arguably mostly pure in their intentions, harbor perverse ambitions that can derail any seemingly good plans. Reinhold Niebuhr offers that a glance at human history proves that "no matter how high the human mind may

---

4. Niebuhr, *The Kingdom*, 193.

reach, there is no level of human moral or social achievement in which there is not some corruption of inordinate self-love."[5]

The fatal flaw of both legalism and relativism, therefore, is idealism. These ideologies rely too much on human achievement while turning a blind eye to self-interest. Today's polarities may very well represent a harsh break with the high view of God handed down through the Reformation. Perhaps this is why liberals may have such a hard time providing realistic checks on people in power. Why have checks and balances when temptation, will-to-power, and sin can be written off as merely slight mistakes among the most learned and cultured among us?[6] It also seems that legalism and relativism both intend to free people, but they actually enslave other by promising perfectibility through human effort.

Christian Realism, driven by radical monotheism, is quite critical of both conservative and liberal Christianity. It invites both conservative and liberal believers to temper their attitudes and actions with a more realistic and balanced approach to human sin and finitude. For instance, we submit that a socialized gospel is and forever will be unable to bring about a utopian state because of human sin. While realists are all for progress and justice in our society, we know that with more progress comes more problems. The social gospel also is more anthropocentric than Christ-centric, meaning that many social justice practices ultimately fall short of God's glory by putting more focus on people's opinions rather than on Jesus Christ.

In other words, the social gospel, seems to have a tendency to be much more social than it is gospel. While social justice may be a worthy endeavor, and practiced with fervent labor, it will be unable to bring about the kind of transformation for which many Christians are ultimately looking. This fact simply is what is. The revelation of Jesus Christ therefore becomes paramount when we consider ways of moving away from the popular liberal/conservative divide among both Christians and Americans today. A reorientation process may be needed for defection from these popular, polarized camps. Such a process is described below through a phased approach.

5. Niebuhr, *Children of Light and Darkness*, 17.
6. Niebuhr, *Children of Light and Darkness*, 45–46.

Reorientation Process Phase 1: Reject Henotheism

Now that we have a modicum of context, we can suggest a process for reorienting ourselves to radical monotheism and thus to Christian Realism. We argue here that the reorientation process occurs in two phases. The first phase involves rejecting henotheism. In the 1700s, Friedrich Shelling coined the term henotheism to describe what happens when some say that they exclusively follow one deity while leaving room open for following popular cultural trends and idols.[7] For the Christian, an idol is any person or thing to which/whom we give our allegiance either alongside or even over God. Henotheism therefore is the belief in one God, but it keeps open the door to worship other things like rules, popular people, power, pride, politics, or whatever else is given some sort of religious, mystical, or divine status by others.

For example, some Christians mistakenly give much allegiance to his/her nation or pop culture over God, all the while claiming that they love God exclusively. The more popular voices of both the Right and Left seem to dictate how people ought to live, replacing the role which is to be reserved only for the Holy Spirit. This is one of the reasons why many people have such a struggle in America determining what is right and wrong. We have perhaps followed too many idols in our social groups, and the most powerful people in these groups try to take God's place and define anything they wish as right or wrong, regardless of reality. These popular people also try to get us to place limits on who can and cannot be our friends and neighbors.

A radical monotheist however realizes that everything we say and do should be done as if Jesus were right in front of us or is even embodied in the person with whom we are interacting. Jesus said that whatever we do to the least loved of all people we have also done to him. Treating people in the way of Christ seems much more realistic and rewarding than the tactics of the Right or Left.

---

7. Niebuhr, *Radical Monotheism*, 58–63.

Reorientation Process Phase 2: Confess Biblical Truth through the Four R's

One may easily fall prey to henotheism if he or she fails to ponder critically upon the truth of the Biblical revelation. Christian Realists affirm the existence of absolute truth, even though we do not claim to know the entire truth due to our humanity. We thereby reject relativism because we believe all truth claims can be and should be tested. We have faith in the truth embodied and revealed in the Lord Jesus Christ. Where we fall short in knowing the truth, we seek new light to come forth from the Bible as the Holy Spirit points out such. Ours is a faith that seeks understanding.

Consequently, if radical monotheism is the engine for Christian Realism, then our confession of biblical truth does the work of the pistons. The admission of biblical truth involves our humble affirmation of our human fallibility, but it also asserts that Jesus Christ is Lord in every aspect, attitude, and action of a Christian's life. We are talking here about being Christian Realists who are radically monotheistic, and we express our exclusive devotion to God by living out of a humbly confessional theology while holding human fallibility and eschatological victory in tension.

There are four primary characteristics of confessional, biblical truth for a Christian Realist, all of which act as fuel for the engine of radical monotheism. We will refer to these characteristics as "The Four R's," known as revelation, relationships, responsibility, and robust Kingdom understanding. When these characteristics work in tandem, a combustible reaction occurs which propels a believer on the narrow way of walking as Jesus walked.

Revelation is the first characteristic of radically monotheistic, biblical truth. Revelation refers to how God reveals details about God's Self to us. Thus, in Jesus Christ, we find a perfect display of what God is like as well as God's will for humankind. Jesus is God in the flesh. Thus, Jesus Christ makes every idea about God more understandable. He answers all our questions about God and makes those blurry ideas about God—those we see as through a dim glass—come into better focus.

For instance, we recently discussed the characteristics of legalists and the relativists. The revelation of God through Jesus Christ helps us to understand how to avoid getting entangled too much in the ideas of these two groups, or at least how to hold them in a better tension. What God has revealed about himself in Jesus Christ helps us to understand God better and to know what it means to look more like Jesus rather than like a rule stickler or relativist.

The second characteristic of our confessed biblical truth deals with how Christians develop effective relationships with unbelievers in their surrounding culture. Conservatives often see conversion as the answer to all the problems of culture, while liberals see activism as the answer. These views are overly one-sided. Christian Realism proposes that we walk exactly as Jesus walked in relationships to others. Christian Realism's practical theology therefore confesses that Christians can neither totally escape nor reject their given culture. So, some believers may be too quick to hand-pick certain Christian doctrines that seem to apply best to what they deem as most appropriate in any given societal context, thus shutting the door on any type of positive spiritual reform or change.

Responsibility is the third main characteristic of biblical truth. Responsibility means more than simply behaving in a culturally acceptable manner around our neighbors. Responsibility balances one's goals and duties with whatever action best represents the way of Jesus in any given situation. Simply put, responsibility asks, "What is the most fitting thing I can do to love God and love my neighbor in this situation, even if that action doesn't exactly fit into a legalistic or relativistic box?"

Take the drinking of alcohol, for instance. A great number of Christian conservatives can be dogmatic about our not drinking, and many may even construct rules to prohibit or shame believers who drink adult beverages. Meanwhile, many liberals or relativists would see nothing wrong with alcohol at all. They may even shame Christians or pressure them into exercising their "Christian freedom" to drink.

Responsible, radical monotheists have a different take. We recognize that, indeed, there are some situations in which it would be perfectly fine for a Christian to consume alcohol while paying attention to the biblical mandate to avoid drunkenness. Yet, there are other situations where the most responsible and loving thing to do requires the Christian to abstain from alcohol to keep a fellow Christian from stumbling into drunkenness or other sins. To be responsible is not centered on rules or adapting to a popular group. It is to answer the question, "What is the most fitting action in view of biblical truth?"[8]

The fourth primary characteristic of our confessed biblical truth is the robust understanding of the Kingdom of God. We can say with great certainty that Jesus' life, ministry, and teaching focused primarily on the Kingdom of God. Consequently, Jesus did not endorse, revolutionize, or overthrow any political or world system during his earthly ministry. This point is especially important for Christian liberals and conservatives. Many liberals could say that Jesus' ministry was focused primarily on social justice, while many conservatives could say that Jesus focused more on getting people to heaven when they die than much else. When liberals and conservatives say such things, they attempt to use Jesus for their own ends. But Jesus cannot be hemmed in by the most popular cultural axioms of the day. His central message concerned the Kingdom. Ours must, too.

Radically monotheistic Christians, then, may find it more life-giving to concern themselves centrally with the Kingdom of God and go to great lengths to put the priorities of God's Kingdom absolutely first in their lives. The task of making God's Kingdom central to one's life is greatly complicated however by the fact that many American Christians today are prodded from church and political leaders to make a choice only between liberalism and conservatism. Yet, radically monotheistic Christians can opt for another option: Seek first the Kingdom of God even if it causes us to be excluded.

Why is the Kingdom of God so important? Because we have no other king than Jesus, and therefore, we do not seek political power to coerce others to fit our agenda. We find that in earthly kingdoms, a leader's rule is limited and subject to sinfulness. God's rule however is unlimited and totally victorious over Satan. Why

8. Niebuhr, *The Responsible Self*, 67.

then would we want to have anything to do with the world's systems other than to love all people within such systems and invite them to join God's Kingdom? True freedom may be most closely identified as we serve as citizens of the Kingdom of God, cutting all ties to the world's systems, and therefore functioning as ambassadors of Christ among the kingdoms of this world.

So. what exactly is the Kingdom of God? This is a good question since the Kingdom sadly may not be the subject of much discussion in American churches and religions today, although there has been a recent resurgence in interest. In fact, we would highly recommend books, videos, and podcasts by Scot McKnight, Greg Boyd, Dallas Willard, N.T. Wright, and Gordon Fee concerning the Kingdom of God for a much richer and fuller discussion than the one here.

In a nutshell, God's kingdom is exactly what it says it is: the realm over which God is King. God, through Abraham, chose a people that would represent God's Kingdom to the world. Many times, however, Abraham's descendants fell into something called "apostasy," which means rejecting God. A Messiah (a word for one who rescues) was desperately needed to free people from their sins. Jesus is this deliverer or Messiah. The gospel, or good news of the Kingdom, is that Jesus died for our sins, was buried, and God raised him from the dead on the third day.

There will come a day called "The Day of the Lord" when God's rule will be universally recognized, and those who reject Jesus will be judged. Jesus alone will rescue people from sin and pronounce them innocent on that Day. Jesus rules by saving people and governing as Lord.

Jesus himself taught much on the Kingdom since he was and is the King. For instance, Jesus taught that repentance is necessary because the coming of the Kingdom on earth as it is in heaven is immanent. Repentance is the act of turning around from the direction on which one is heading that is contrary to the way of Jesus Christ and thus walking on a pilgrimage through life that obeys and learns from Jesus as his disciple, or student. We get into the Kingdom based on obedience to God's will. Perfect obedience is not possible, however, on human terms. There's nothing we can do to earn or achieve perfect obedience. Surrender to Christ by trust, or faith, is the only way to get our lives right with God. In a sense, salvation is the surrender and death of our ego in order to offer full allegiance to Jesus Christ for the rest of our lives. To become a citizen of the kingdom of God is to submit wholly to Jesus Christ as the one true God and King. His grace saves us. Thus, the Kingdom takes precedence over everything else in our lives.

The local church has an important role in the Kingdom of God, too. Jesus created the church. He referred to it as the "ecclesia," a simple Greek term that means something like "the called-out ones," or "the assembly of people for a set purpose." The church is the entity set up by Christ to proclaim and teach about the Kingdom. Churches are somewhat like local embassies for the kingdom among the nations of the world. It is important to note that early members of the ecclesia were not called Christians. The term "Christian" was first used in a place called Antioch, years after the church was originally formed. The original term used for Christians was "Followers of the Way," or even simply "The Way."

Wouldn't it be something if Christians could be known today more for being followers of the Way of Jesus and emissaries for the Kingdom of God than for their politics and entrenchment in the ways of the kingdoms of this world? This is why radically monotheistic Christians attempt to focus much more of their time and effort on prioritizing the kingdom of God in their lives and church involvement. We view the Kingdom of God as the utmost treasure to be discovered and cherished for all time. Accordingly, we desire to be Followers of the Way even if that runs counter to liberalism and conservatism and the popularity created in the world when Christians give themselves over to the two primary worldly religious camps.

Implementing the Reorientation Phases with The Balanced Approach

Let's get even more specific now by examining concise and understandable ways to implement the two phases of reorienting oneself to radical monotheism. We implement the two reorientation phases by utilizing what we call "The Balanced Approach" to the Christian life. The Balanced Approach may be defined as that which is not limited by the either/or choices of legalism and relativism. We rather opt for a both/and approach to balance the nature of our Christian faith with its realistic application in the complexities of the world. In other words, adaptation to some degree to the world can lead to a more profound impact for Christ that the given polarities. We are to be both in the world and not of the world.

The Balanced Approach consists then of two primary action steps. We will briefly name these action steps here and then expound upon them in some detail in forthcoming chapters. The first step is to realize our own limitations and subsequently offer grace to others. Can we confess that we are often involved in the same sins that we judgmentally call out in others? Like it or not, we are all neighbors, so why not serve one another in humility rather than through the one-upmanship of legalism or through the toleration of sin through relativism? There is always something more to learn, to glean, or to confess as we acknowledge sins of omission and commission. Life is much more than who has the correct rules or who has done the largest number of good deeds. When we realize our sinfulness and accompany this realization with surrendering to the grace of Christ, then we have taken the most important first step in holding both conservatism and liberalism in tension through a more realistic approach.

The second reorienting step is to take oneself out of conservative and/or liberal camps. We do not have to play their games. For example, consider the social justice movement of more liberal Christians. In the Christian tradition, social justice usually refers to the bringing the Kingdom of God to earth as it is perceived to be functioning in heaven. Specifically, social justice refers to bringing about fair and morally decent relationships in a given society, including but not limited to redistribution of wealth and creating avenues for restorative justice to occur to those who have been wronged by both imperialists and those who have held the most power in a society for a significant period of time. Social justice activists highly value what they deem as the common good.

While social justice can greatly aid us while serving our neighbors with humility, we should also balance and temper our approach by realizing the sinfulness in our own spiritual DNA. Put simply, we should always be wary of our confidence to know what is always best for everyone.

Further, how do we know for sure that economic redistribution and cozying up to the powers that be on the left or right sides of the political aisle is actually kingdom work? The Balanced Approach is rather skeptical of the motives of those who try to justify the common good through ideology. We recognize the benevolence of those on both the Right and the Left, but we also recognize the limits to such benevolence in the face of basic human corruption. Christian Realists assert that the Kingdom of God will come on earth as it is in heaven not through political power but only through our prayerful surrender to Christ and his grace.

Through a reorientation process, we also may come to recognize that we have no ready-made answers to the questions being asked in our culture today. Yet, The Balanced Approach can rid us of the overbearing legalism of the conservative Right and the utopian henotheism of the progressive Left in order that we may seek first the Kingdom of God. Jesus is the ultimate Revelation who makes all other revelations and truth statements sensible. Apart from Jesus Christ, we can do nothing.

The following chapters elaborate on the reorienting steps of The Balanced Approach. When we follow these steps, we can begin to apply and implement a formidable and helpful Christian Realism solution to the many complex and fear-filled problems in today's Western culture.

2

The Balanced Approach Step One

Realize Limitations and Offer Grace to Each Other

The Christian Realism solution simply cannot exist without humility. Humility exists at the heart of any action one takes to overcome the limitations of the legalistic Right and relativistic Left. Humility arises as one adds to his/her understanding of human nature from a biblical perspective. Reinhold Niebuhr and Emil Brunner, both celebrated and influential Christian theologians, help us a great deal at this point. Let's extract some main ideas from their career work to help us step forward in humility towards the Christian Realism solution.

Humility and Human Nature: Appreciating Reinhold Niebuhr

Reinhold Niebuhr's brand of Christian Realism asserts that that every person, due to sin, acts out of their own self-interest. Self-interest is defined here as that which drives a person to put on pretenses, or faces, to show how much better they are than others. Thus, submission to God through Christ is the only way to overcome the ego in any sort of ultimate sense.

The inclination towards the more acute forms of self-interest in the Western world, particularly among Americans, has been shaped primarily by our Greco-Roman heritage. Niebuhr specifically argues that our Hellenistic heritage produced two highly influential views about humanity which still have relevance primarily in the West. These two views function essentially as two sides of one coin. The first view is called the Classical View, while the other is known as the Contemporary View.[1]

The Classical View, rooted mainly in the teachings of Plato and Aristotle, posits that the human spirit and body are separate. The human mind is given higher value than the body. The mind is also given higher priority because it can think thoughts which go beyond physical boundaries. For instance, we can imagine ourselves floating in space or swimming in the depths of the ocean while never leaving the couch. We can also meditate on great theories of wisdom without ever taking our bodies anywhere. Even the most physically disabled person can transcend limitations of the body within his/her mind.

Although mental transcendence is a wonderful trait of human life, Christian Realists argue that those who adhere to the Classical View tend to become henotheistic, with higher reasoning skills becoming a god or idol. Reason and mental intelligence can easily be viewed as the gateway to immortality—the mind being that which lives on even though the body dies. While there is virtually no consideration of an after-life in the Classic View, the mind is said to go on living in some sort of state. Think John Lennon's song, "Instant Karma." We all shine on. While this thinking may drive contemporary art, it has little to offer in terms of engaging reality.

Niebuhr rightly argues that two ancient Roman groups adhered to the Classical View, and their ideas still exact a strong influence in contemporary Western culture. One group, the Stoics, taught that the mind can and must have power over the body, especially through the practice of taming emotions and showing little preference for joy or happiness. The second group, the Epicureans, had some similar beliefs to the Stoics with the exception

1. Niebuhr, *The Nature and Destiny of Man*, 1–25.

that they heartily embraced the impulses of the body more than the Stoics. If the mind could not overcome or control some aspects of the physical body, then it would be best to allow whatever practices which promote the best experiences of happiness. Epicureanism basically does its best to fulfill the axiom, "Eat, drink, and be merry, for tomorrow we die."

The biblical view of radical Christian monotheism obviously differs greatly from the Classical View. The Bible teaches that God created humanity in the image of God, complete with bodies and minds which function in tandem. A human being is thus an autonomous heart, soul, mind, and strength which function in unison. The image of God means then that God gave humans freedom to use our highly developed minds and bodies in responsible ways.

Sin, of course, defaced the image of God in us. Consequently, God's revelation through Jesus Christ illustrates how we are to understand ourselves as human beings and be reconciled with God. In Christ we learn that God loves us, died for us, and intends to reconcile with us. In other words, we are to be in relationship with God, not to achieve divinity in our own right. We are all sinners in need of God's grace.

This brings us to the Contemporary View of human nature. Niebuhr writes that the Contemporary View is basically a form of the Classical View filtered through the extensive philosophical uproars of the Renaissance and Enlightenment periods. It rests upon Rene Descartes's axiom, "I think, therefore I am." Descartes's snowball of a thought developed into an avalanche of philosophical propositions, the most prominent being both Rationalism and Romanticism. These suggest that the human mind, freed from the limitations of the body, has nearly limitless potential. Human evil and sin are downplayed as that which comes from the natural impulses of the body. Such impulses are said to be overcome by free, enlightened, and disciplined, positive thinking.

The Contemporary View goes by any number of names in today's American culture, chief of which is Progressivism, or the idea that human beings are always moving towards some sort of idealistic, utopian society in which most, if not all problems and challenges will be trumped by an educated, enlightened, and unified world community. Some progressives therefore view Christianity as entirely cynical and thus irrelevant due to its emphasis on sin and seeking first the Kingdom of God. Yet, those progressive people who see at least some value in Christianity may attempt to coopt Christian faith and practice by lessening the impact of biblical emphases on sin.

In fact, Progressivism and Christianity can often make strange bedfellows. Progressive Christianity seems to fixate upon the power of the human spirit to overcome limitations, generally argued with a phrase like, "You can do anything you set your mind to." Some of the more prominent, upscale megachurches in America today seem to have attached the Contemporary View to Christianity. Christian Realists however confess that it is a grave error to conclude that human reason can be equal to the Spirit of God.

It is ironic that liberal mainline churches are essentially operating out of the same mindset as some prosperity gospel preachers, but such are the impacts of the Contemporary View. We must remember that human creativity and rational thinking should never be linked to human divinity. Just because we are created in the image of God does not mean that we are becoming divine in some way. Human nature remains vastly overrated and fallible before the holy Lord.

Yet, there have been some progressives of the Contemporary View who eventually realized that everything was not right with human reason. Instead of turning to God, however, usually a boogie man is chosen and blamed for hampering the utopian vision. Karl Marx is likely the most outspoken of such progressives to date. He scapegoated the privileged, powerful, and oppressive bourgeois for creating massive physical and economic disparities.

Marx was definitely onto something when he concluded that human materialistic power cannot be sufficiently checked by reason. Marx and his ilk, however, committed a substantial error by failing to recognize one of the most obvious tenants of realism: people from all economic levels function out of self-interest. Human evil and will-to-power is no respecter of persons. Marx's advocacy of reorganizing society to improve or eliminate disparities among the privileged and non-privileged classes will simply never work due to the fact that his system depends on supposedly more reasonable people to guide the process. Marx essentially created a system that is no better than the ones he critiqued. Niebuhr bluntly says, "Their (Marxists') cynicism doesn't save them from their stupidity."[2] He further concludes, "The social substance of life is richer and more various, and has greater depths and tensions than are envisaged in the Marxist dream of social harmony."[3]

Simply put, Marx's ideology was an illusion. We human beings cannot simply overcome racial, economic, and class gaps by reeducating the masses or offering some form of redemption from our history. In order for a Marxist program to work today, its advocates would have to show how the evils in Capitalism or Colonialism came about in the first place. If one took a dive deep enough into history, he/she would find the rudimentary element of human sin and self-interest pervades whatever system it is in question.

Radically monotheistic Christian Realists however view that while all people are definitely created equal, there is a flaw in every single one of us, which is the tendency towards emphasizing our rights over our responsibilities. Responsibility is ultimately on the shoulders of the individual since Jesus primarily saw people in terms of their individuality. Accordingly, any change begins with looking at ourselves in the mirror and, more importantly, placing ourselves in repentance before a holy God, no matter how pure we believe our motives to be.

Put more concretely, the gods of nature, reason, and even science collapse under the weight of our sin. There can be no such thing as an ideal society in which a person becomes divine in nature through their progressive intellectualism. The Rationalism and Romanticism of the Contemporary View will never fully be able to subsume the individual into a collective in which men and women essentially become gods and put aside their desires to dominate one another. Our only hope is reconciliation with Jesus Christ and understanding our true rights and responsibilities as individuals as best as is humanly possible.

2. Niebuhr, *The Children of Light and Darkness*, 32.
3. Niebuhr, *The Children of Light and Darkness*, 59.

Suffice it to say, not all people in the West adhere to the Classic view, the Contemporary view, or the Christian view of human nature. Some simply take on a kind of cynical apoplexy about the deeper problems and disparities of life. This usually results in a person attempting to make his or herself as comfortable as possible with entertaining distractions until death. Others may try to fool themselves by translating their pessimism into some sort of positive view that at some point all human beings will be able somehow to get along eventually.[4] It appears as though some simply refuse to deal with any reality as a coping mechanism for their anxieties surrounding sin and death.

Christians may still be hopeful, but not because of some higher form of reasoning or because we place trust in our ability to reorganize society in our image. Rather, our hope is in Christ Jesus. The Christian view, in opposition to the Classic and Contemporary views of our Greco-Roman forebears, comes to terms with the truth that all people sin and fall short of the glory of God. We find no other alternative and authoritative norm for life than to submit ourselves to the will and way God through the only mediator between God and humankind—Jesus Christ. We find any attempt at exalting our minds and spiritual creativity to a point to where we lose touch with both ourselves and reality is superfluous, and we therefore opt to proclaim with the Psalmist that God's thoughts are not ours. Consequently, we believe that the human mind is finite and restless until finding a much more restful home in reconciled relationship with God.

How then shall we live? Niebuhr would likely suggest that humankind must come to terms with our own sin. But what is sin? Classic, Contemporary, and even Christian thinkers would all likely have many divergent definitions. For instance, a Contemporary philosopher like Hegel would offer that sin is a matter of making a simple error against one's goals. Hegel would therefore suggest that some sins could be beneficial or good in that they point the way to better achievement and appropriation of ambition. Hegel's theology supports such a view, as he likened God to a clock maker

---

4. Niebuhr, *Nature and Destiny*, 49–53.

who winds up history and allows time to spin without much divine input. Those who sin and atone for it on their own can put themselves in a position to beat the clock.[5] It's a "may best person win" kind of theology.

Christian Realists can rely more completely on Scripture for a concise and helpful explanation of sin than any other viewpoint. The biblical record of both human history and God's revelation in Christ suggests that human sin is primarily a missing of the mark, or complete lack of fulfilling the will of God, both intentionally or unintentionally. Niebuhr offers that since humankind can think outside the box while also kicking against the pricks of our finiteness, we tend to become anxious at our limitations. The anxiety caused by our recognition of finitude opens a door for temptation or attempting to deny God the rightful place of Creator, Redeemer, and Sustainer.[6]

Niebuhr also argues that pride and sensuality seem to be the most basic of sins, which becomes especially important in pointing out the errors of both Classic and Contemporary Views. Pride, as defined by Niebuhr, is that which either denies one's finitude or attempts to escape it. Niebuhr asserts that pride has three primary types, or expressions: the pride of power, the pride of intellect, and the pride of moral superiority.[7]

The sin of sensuality can be closely linked to pride, for it includes more than sexual perversity. Sensuality seems to be driven more by the power of lust and, to larger degree, by a selfish type of inward-focused love. When it comes to sensuality, the self is supposed to get whatever the self wants.

Societies impacted greatly by Classic and Contemporary ideologies do not seem to handle the sin of sensuality well. In fact, many people in the West seem to have bought into the notion that sensuality is not much of a sin at all, if it is even a sin to begin with. The notion that most people have been repressed as to their sexual identity and expressions descends from the Epicurean tradition of

5. Niebuhr, *Nature and Destiny*, 116–17.

6. Niebuhr, *The Nature and Destiny*, 168.

7. Niebuhr, *The Nature and Destiny*, 186–203.

thought. Progressives have simply picked up on the notion that the body has sensual and sexual impulses about which the mind should adapt rather than tame or jettison. We would be hard pressed, for instance, to find many progressives who would agree with Jesus' teaching to cut off the eye or arm that causes one to lust. Progressive thought would also likely suggest that Jesus modify his teaching to redefine "lust" in ways that are less repressive to that which is deemed to be our natural inclinations.

Jesus however is clear that sensuality has more to do with the heart than what we commonly consider, meaning that a relaxation on sexual restraints will do little, if anything, to improve society. Niebuhr suggests that lustful sex is either an escape of ego through using another or the assertion of ego in dominance over another.[8] Christian Realists agree then with Jesus that neither repression nor relaxation of sensuality does anyone any good. When one begins however to poke out the eye which causes him or her to lust, significant death of the ego takes place and makes room for a more meaningful expression of sexuality to occur in which participants in a sexual union find life by dying to self.

Consider however the ways in which modern, or postmodern, society takes a rather dim view of Christian challenges to the sins of pride and sensuality. This is due to a penchant to blame society's ills on institutions and cultural traditions than on selfish pride or lust. Christian Realists therefore advocate for losing life in order to find it. Niebuhr says it like this: "The highest self-realization is the subjection of man's particular will to universal will of God."[9]

Expressing Humility through what is Fair and Good: Appreciating Emil Brunner

At this point that we find the work of Niebuhr's colleague, Emil Brunner, highly appealing and relevant to our exploration of humility as it pertains to the radical monotheism of Christian Realism. Brunner rarely, if ever, used the exact terminology of the Niebuhr

8. Niebuhr, *The Nature and Destiny*, 236–37.
9. Niebuhr, *The Nature and Destiny*, 252.

brothers, yet his ideas bear a striking commonality with the Niebuhrs' radical monotheism. In fact, Brunner's seminal volume, *The Divine Imperative*, spells out a practical form of radical monotheism that adds to the flavor of what we have already discussed. Some of Brunner's main ideas will be addressed here, particularly as to how they apply directly to living with humility by recognizing one's faults and offering grace to others.

One of Brunner's chief concerns is with how and why humans define and ultimately do that which is right, fair, or good. He would likely view our culture's casual definition of the common good as especially problematic. More often than not, our society sees the common good as that which a large number of people do as it is defined by the majority. This definition unwisely puts the reigns of defining good within the grasp of whatever political party or economic group in power sees as good, no matter how harmful or unrealistic that good may be.

Choosing to do the good and ordering life based on God's grace is often referred to as Christian ethics. A simple definition of Christian ethics is taking action in everyday relationships from a Christian perspective. Christian ethics naturally differs from other ethical systems which are based on Classical and Contemporary Views. In fact, Brunner cautions us especially against what he called naturalistic ethics and idealistic ethics.

Naturalistic ethics describe a system of behaviors that comes from one's attempt at satisfying his/her individual happiness. Such a system of morality would propose that all ethics stem from natural truths. In other words, a naturalistic person could say, "It's natural for me to do or feel like this, therefore, I will behave in a certain manner according to my natural feelings." Arguments in favor of certain prideful or sensual sins are usually based in naturalistic ethics. The mantra, "If it feels good, do it," effectively encapsulates naturalistic ethics.

Idealistic ethics deal less with personal happiness and more with what are called the oughts of life. It coincides well with the Classic View of Stoicism. In fact, idealist ethics sound like what it is—an attempt to behave based only on what we ought to do in any given situation. One's sense of individuality is accordingly subordinated to the ideals of the group in power. Idealism springs more from the classical Stoic thought in which the supposedly reasonable, enlightened mind suppresses emotion and natural impulses of the body in order to establish and subsequently accomplish the greater good.[10]

There are obviously occasions when both naturalistic ethics and idealistic ethos run amok. For instance, naturalism can often spin into a hideous kind of materialism and hedonism. When such occurs, ethics become relativized, and that which is deemed responsible behavior is based merely on the psychology of an individual and/or the emotions of that individual. We could even argue here that the entire philosophical system called postmodernity is a perversion of naturalistic ethics.

In postmodern thought, truth is said to be subjective, or relative to the thoughts and feelings of an individual or powerful group. It explains much of the confusion surrounding the ethics of gender and sexuality in the West today. We are told that if one feels like or thinks like another gender, then it must be so. The culture then encourages them to become what they feel. Such a relativizing of objective truth however can have disastrous consequences for a society which lacks any point of reference for behavior other than natural, and therefore sinful, impulses which are essentially detached from reality.

In Christianity, therefore, the good is accomplished neither through obeying natural impulses nor by always doing what we ought in order to fulfill some biased religio-cultural behavioral narrative. We base our behaviors not upon a philosophy or principle, but upon a Person. We recognize good as the will of God. The will of God ultimately is revealed in the life, death, and resurrection of Christ: Love of God and love of neighbor is therefore the ultimate good worth our pursuit.

Notice also that both naturalistic and idealistic ethics place human beings at the core of life, or as the ultimate Value Center. A neighbor in this philosophy becomes the means to our ends. Faith in Christ opens the eyes of a person to understand that God

10. Brunner, *The Divine Imperative*, 34–44.

is the center of life and being—the Subject of life, not an Object.[11] By faith, we become woven into the fabric of God's purposes and empowered not by the self but by the Holy Spirit to obey God. All of life is that of God's grace. We can say with confidence then that the love of Christ which directs and compels us is in total the end of life and the basis for all ethics of the good. We can only be and do good as it comes from God's action in and through us.

But how do we know exactly what is the good will of God? How do we hear and process the commands of God? The only basis of knowing and doing God's will is by receiving instruction from the Holy Spirit.[12] Keep in mind that Jesus through His Spirit is the only intermediary between God and a believer. Since God sent Jesus, this means that God will be faithful to reveal his nature, character, and will to the believer. God desires to deal with each of us personally. Real and true faith is obedience to God and God alone. The primary concern of life therefore is not the satisfaction of one's ego, or the unleashing one's inner god. It is the will of God to whom one's life belongs.

Knowing the will of God begins with our accurately reading the Bible. People sometimes conclude that the Bible is simply a book of rules and prohibitions. Indeed, prohibitions are in the Bible, but it is quite helpful for us to ask about the meaning behind such rules. Can we not conclude that some, if not all, of the prohibitions in the Bible come from God's loving character to protect us from ourselves? Consider how parents prohibit their children from putting their fingers into a power socket. Do parents forbid children from doing what they want to punish them? By no means! They have established certain criteria in their home that the children may flourish. If earthly parents prohibit their children from electrocuting themselves, then how much more does God desire for us to experience God's deeply profound will and grace?

Keep in mind, however, that it is possible to resist God. Just as a child resists the guidance of parents and guardians, so can we turn from the way of the Lord by our own free will. We can put our

11. Brunner, *The Divine Imperative*, 152.

12. Brunner, *The Divine Imperative*, 284–85.

fingers in the light socket despite the best efforts of our parents. In the same way, God sometimes limits his power to allow us to make our choices. This is why it is crucial for us, when we read the Bible, to ask some serious questions about our motivations. What is our self-interest telling us to do when we hear the Lord speak? When God shows us further how to love him to the fullest and to love our neighbors, how do we respond?

In addition to knowing and doing the teachings of the Bible, we can know God's will by applying the principles of the Bible into everyday situations. It's impossible to anticipate every ethical dilemma that we will face, but the commands and demands of Scripture remain constant. They will however be applied in varying ways in varying circumstances. Some people fail to know and do the will of God because there are many occasions when complex decision opportunities arise, mainly due to the arbitrariness of life. All decisions about God's will are not in black and white. In fact, we could argue that the majority of life's dilemmas come to us with a gray color. In order then to make the more difficult decisions about God's will, we must read the Bible and apply the principles thereof in the light of the revelation of Jesus Christ. It is then that we will find the good and the fair and then put it into practice with humility as we engage reality with the clearest conscience possible.[13]

Another of Brunner's main concerns relates to how Christians live in the contemporary tension between individualism and collectivism. Brunner, like Niebuhr, essentially argues that a healthy, biblical view of the individual will lead us to become humbler.[14] For instance, since every person is created in the image of God, those persons not only have the capacity to understand God's Word and God's will, but they also are born with incalculable worth and dignity. Sin has corrupted us to such a degree however that we have lost the ability to maintain a healthy, humble, graceful balance between individuals and groups without a relationship with God. If we focus too much on the individual, then we will tend to magnify our rights over our responsibilities. And if we focus too much on the collective,

13. Brunner, *The Divine Imperative*, 179–87.

14. Brunner, *The Divine Imperative*, 297–307.

then we will tend to sacrifice the rights of the individual. These are scenarios in which humility and grace become casualties.

Total dependence on God through a reconciled relationship with Christ re-clarifies our sense of value and leads us to value others in appropriate ways.[15] In fact, one of the humbler ways of valuing one another—contrary to popular opinion on both the Right and the Left—is the truth that, while all people are created equal, there are certain inequalities of function. For example, a person who is barely five feet tall and has little athletic skill is unequal in function to a nearly seven foot person who can play basketball on a professional level. The teachings of the Bible clearly indicate an inequality of function, for the church is said to be one body with many parts. A hand cannot be an eye, but the hand is not allowed to devalue the eye simply because of functional inequality. Rather, functional inequality opens the door to a humble recognition that we are all different while still being of unique worth.

When either individuals or a collective fails to recognize inequality of function, they will eventually value rights over responsibilities or responsibilities over rights. Keep in mind however that Jesus primarily focused on the rights and responsibilities of the individual before he focused on crowds. He said, in fact, that he would build his church based on the confession of his Lordship by individuals. Jesus builds the church from individuals, not a collective. He focused on a proper balance of rights and responsibilities. Such a balance is possible only through humble engagement with one's neighbor.[16]

But we may ask, "What are my rights and responsibilities?" Despite our functional inequalities, there are certain rights afforded by God alone to every person created in His image. These rights naturally come with tremendous responsibilities. If we were to focus too much on our rights, then we would abrogate our humility and consequently harm our neighbor. For instance, one such inalienable right from God is the right of conscience.[17] Every individual

---

15. Brunner, *The Divine Imperative*, 220–48.

16. Brunner, *The Divine Imperative*, 220.

17. Brunner, *The Divine Imperative*, 156–59.

has a right to worship and to live according to the dictates of his/her conscience and not according to coercion from others. Yet, with this right comes the responsibility of self-sacrifice to one's community.

For example, when Jesus mentioned that he laid down his life willingly, he affirmed the right to ownership of his body and conscience, free from coercion of any entity. But he also affirmed the use of body ownership is sacrificial. Could it be that we have a right to be free from domination from others while simultaneously bearing the responsibility to use such freedom in a way that is humbly sacrificial for the sake of our neighbors?

Paul's admonition to the Corinthian Christians to abstain from meat sacrificed to idols gives a similar insight. While individuals in the church had a perfectly sound right to eat such meat, they were called upon not to flaunt their rights but to use them in a responsible way as to not allow their new friends in the faith to stumble or be tempted to sin. Paul refrained from using his either his apostolic privilege or coercion to teach the church about meat sacrificed to idols, as well. His appeal was to their individual consciences as to what the humble, fitting action in the circumstance would be in accordance with the way of Christ. Paul advocated Christian ethics based on reality.

Another inalienable right is the right from domination. Since only God alone is good, then God alone must be considered the ultimate Subject of good conduct. Any system, collective, or even individual who attempts to usurp the position of God, automatically becomes illustrious of evil. Perhaps the best way to achieve better forms of justice in society of unequal function comes only through balancing the rights and responsibilities of individuals in a context of freedom, especially in terms of worship, assembly, speech, and property. Such freedom allows individuals the necessary room to recognize and humbly admit faults while also embracing his/her own unique skills in light of the full gospel of Jesus Christ. In other words, freedom is a breeding ground for faith. We find ourselves able to argue, speak, learn, read, and develop our minds in accordance with God's allowance of our free will.

Yet, we ought to be careful at this point since total freedom would likely result in anarchy. The ancient Greeks, and therefore many Americans, valued freedom from domination basically for self-improvement. The line of thinking goes that if we improve ourselves enough, then we can achieve some sort of perfection or divinity. Christians however are to value freedom from domination for consistent and constant reflection upon and practice of the grace of God in humble reconciliatory actions for our neighbors, not self-improvement alone. Ours is to be a freedom from domination in order to serve others, not to "become what thou art."[18]

In fact, we could argue that simply trying to be a good person is not realistically possible, since all human activity is tainted by sin and self-interest. Full freedom would accordingly result in chaos of primarily self-interested people. Rather, we attend to a journey of becoming better only in the recognition of our finitude and repentance of sin. Being good is living by the law of love as directed by the Holy Spirit of Jesus in the life of the believer. In fact, freedom from domination is the freedom to discover one's true self—a sinner in need of grace. In the words of Niebuhr, it is an "impossible possibility" for humankind to do and be good in the fullest sense until the direct intervention of the Lord upon his imminent return.

So, how do Christians humbly work to take steps towards balancing rights and responsibilities within the down-and-dirty, realistic world in which we live right now? First, we must recognize that humility in its truest sense is not necessarily as much of a human achievement as it is a function of faith. Brunner says that a state of humility "is only possible in a life of faith and therefore in a very different sense from that of ordinary virtue."[19] In other words, we find ourselves growing and practicing humility by renouncing our claim to being totally virtuous people.[20] We may be virtuous in some parts of life while also coming up far short of God's target in others. Consequently, humility comes from our free will choice to obey Christ's command to "follow me" as repentant sinners in need of mercy and grace, since following Jesus results in the denial

18. Brunner, *The Divine Imperative*, 40.

19. Brunner, *The Divine Imperative*, 187.

20. Brunner, *The Divine Imperative*, 179.

of self and the taking up of a cross by the individual's free choice of conscience without any coercion.

Second, we agree with Brunner that life is less about our doing good out of self-interest and is more about doing the good which naturally arises from a reconciled relationship with God through submission to Jesus Christ as we are empowered by the Holy Spirit. Put simply, an apple tree will produce apples not to please itself but because that is simply what an apple tree does. When Jesus says, "I was hungry and you fed me," hopefully our response will come from a place of submission to God's will which inquires, "Lord, when did we do that?" Such a question would be based in our ability through God's Spirit to respond naturally and almost unknowingly to needs around us.

We can conclude then that humility involves the complete sacrifice of one's will to God with the understanding that one's flesh will constantly vie for recognition and will hope to turn one's interests patently inward. In fact, Brunner offers plainly that "to believe" in Christ means, "Don't bother about yourself anymore. God has put your affairs in order."[21] Brunner would even argue that we when we surrender our life to Christ, we essentially have just one job—to love God and love neighbor.

Consequently, Brunner advocates for a kind of reductionism of the self which actually opposes the construction of what he calls "ideological programs."[22] In other words, there is reason to posit no other solutions to the central issues of human life other than one found in Jesus Christ. All other human attempts at bringing in some sort of nirvana-like order ultimately collapse under the weight of human nature and fallenness. There can truly be no sort of order in life other than the law of love.

But what about reforms to the church and to the world? Are we supposed to be passive believers just doing the best we can until the Lord returns? By no means. Humility is not equal to passivity. What we are suggesting is that the Lord's order, found in submission to Christ as King, is the ultimate standard by which we should

---

21. Brunner, *The Divine Imperative*, 190.
22. Brunner, *The Divine Imperative*, 230.

go about our daily business. God has given us talents for use in his service. Burying our talents in the ground is akin to spiritual suicide. Yet, all actions we take should be measured in accordance to the law of love. Just doing something for the sake of activity, or living in total accord with the cultural status quo, is irrelevant at best and prideful at worst.

A passive withdrawal from the culture negatively impacts the witness of the church in the world. The means with which we accomplish our ends as Christians requires humble and tactful concern for cooperating with others around us from the point at which they are, not the point we would like for them to be. It may be more realistic then to aim for the best justice and economic systems possible for our time as ambassadors rather than waiting around for the Day of the Lord. In doing so with humility, we will find that "the most personal thing of all is not doing something for love, but showing love."[23]

23. Brunner, *The Divine Imperative*, 278.

3

Step Two

Removal from Conservative and Liberal Camps

The Balanced Approach, or reorientation process of Christian Realism, not only includes humility, but it also places a tremendous emphasis on an individual removing oneself from becoming entrenched in both conservative and liberal camps. A significant effort to avoid entrenchment in one of these partisan political or religious groups is both quite admirable and possible for the realist.

At first glance however we may find that any attempt at removal from these groups may appear to be vain at best and impossible at worst. We are not suggesting that someone attempt to withdraw from the world to such a point that he/she forfeits a say in the political conversations of the day. Far from it. Christian Realists can become quite comfortable with political involvement. Yet, we are talking about how to approach life, faith, and politics from a macro level instead of a micro one. Removal from both conservative and liberal camps often involves viewing reality from a 35,000 foot-level instead of at the height of a crop-duster. Macro politics helps one get at particularly important and ultimate life issues from a steadier and healthier perspective, without taking immediate sides on an issue before proper investigation.

We are thus talking about refusal to believe everything one hears and reads, even if such information comes from the most trusted sources. Christian Realists promote testing all the spirits. For faith truly to be faith, then one must test everything—even faith itself. The conservative and liberal biases concerning our societal value centers and ultimate issues ought to be tested constantly. Questioning the status quo should be welcomed and encouraged, even at the cost of expulsion from one's in-crowd.

Paul Tillich's descriptions of faith and doubt may become particularly helpful at this point. Tillich defines faith as "the state of being ultimately concerned."[1] For the Christian, God is to be one's ultimate concern, not the dictates of popular social groups or those who wield the sword. Tillich argues, "In true faith, the ultimate concern is a concern about the truly ultimate; while in idolatrous faith preliminary, finite realities are elevated to the rank of ultimacy."[2] In other words, when we elevate legalism, relativism, and their cognates to the level of ultimacy for our lives, we have committed the sin of idolatry. The elevation of that which is finite to the level of being infinite is not only a rejection of reality, but it is also a cowardly act. In fact, true courage comes to the forefront of our lives when we embrace uncertainty in our faith in Christ. Uncertainty, in this case, does not mean that one is rendered useless by the indecision. Rather, uncertainty is a way of saying, "Christ is my ultimate concern in spite of this or that."[3]

We can thereby argue that doubt is a "confirmation of faith."[4] Doubt and uncertainty help us to question all the answers, to examine all definitions of reality. While conservatives and liberals may criticize us for doubting and questioning their narratives, our faith in the true way of Jesus Christ gives us the courage to become more serious about ultimate concerns in life. We cannot afford to accept lock, stock, and barrel the hypotheses of those who wish us to buy

---

1. Tillich, *Dynamics of Faith*, 1.
2. Tillich, *Dynamics of Faith*, 12.
3. Tillich, *Dynamics of Faith*, 21.
4. Tillich, *Dynamics of Faith*, 22.

into their lines of thinking. To buy into a hypothesis is not faith.[5] In fact, we can argue that most legalists and relativists desire for us to put our faith in many of their hypotheses which contradict reality. Faith is neither a belief in something nor is it agreement to some sort of demands made upon us by legalists or relativist. Faith is "concern about what is experienced as ultimate."[6] Therefore, faith is that which does not just believe in reality but it doubts, researches, pokes, prods, and elevates reality since faith sees and experiences the presence of God in reality.

So, what does this mean in everyday action? In a nutshell, removing oneself from groups of people who tend to get emotional and red-faced even during cursory viewing of either Fox News or CNN is highly recommended. By "removal," we do not mean total withdrawal or some kind of holier-than-thou attitude. Removal refers to cutting ties, not with people, but with ideas that would tend to keep one relegated to one specific political and theological camp. Keep in mind that we are talking about The Balanced Approach, a way of being in the world without becoming of the world. Since Jesus commanded Christians to make disciples of all nations, including people of all political and religious persuasions, we understand Christ to mean that we ought to be more realistic about the idolatrous interests of individuals and groups around us.

It may be helpful here to consider Jesus as our North Star when it comes to standard operating procedure in making disciples, not our political bents. One of the reasons why Jesus was able to move well in diverse crowds of people so effectively seems to have more to do with his penchant to care more for people and their ultimate problems than for the spirit of his era. So, we are not speaking about removing our fellowship from people. Jesus welcomed crowds of people from all different walks of life and only retreated for times of prayer, reflection, and training of small groups of disciples. Our stand is not against people but against the powers and principalities at work around all of us. Could it be that the politics and religious persuasions of the Left and Right are more akin to principalities

5. Tillich, *Dynamics of Faith*, 33.
6. Tillich, *Dynamics of Faith*, 9.

than to anything of eternal worth from God? There are living, breathing people behind the masks of politico-religious bents. Can we not cut through the masks to care for the person?

Christian Realists therefore may propose a two-tiered approach to taking this macro-political/evangelistic approach to life. The first tier involves argument with the plausibility structures of a given society. Peter Berger, a sociologist, coined the term "plausibility structure" to give some definition to those certain beliefs among groups of people which determine acceptable and unacceptable behavior.[7] That is, whatever is deemed to be reasonable by a majority of a given community is the group's reigning plausibility structure, regardless of whether or not that which is reasonable is also realistic. Lesslie Newbigin discusses plausibility structures of cultures in relationship to Christians at length in his important book, *The Gospel in a Pluralist Society*. He offers that the gospel of Christ is a plausibility structure of its own, yet the Christian plausibility structure is "a radically different vision of things from those that shape all human cultures apart from the gospel."[8] But how so?

Newbigin offers that Christians must learn to operate well between two poles. One pole represents membership in the Kingdom of God in which the language spoken is that of the Bible. The other pole represents the community which speaks a language quite foreign to Scripture and interprets life on much different terms than that of the Kingdom. Newbigin would say that the most realistic response of the Christian could be: "I do not live within that plausibility (American culture), but I know what it feels like to live in it."[9] In other words, we are to understand what it means to inhabit the ethos of both conservative and liberal communities while simultaneously focusing on the telos, or ultimate goal, of the kingdom of God. We are to be in the world but not of the world.[10]

Accordingly, we operate as citizens of the Kingdom as we also live as resident aliens in the world. In this kind of operation, there

---

7. Berger. *The Sacred Canopy*, 12.

8. Newbigin, *Pluralist Society*, 9.

9. Newbigin, *Pluralist Society*, 9.

10. Newbigin, *Pluralist Society*, 9.

will likely be continuous, ongoing argument between the plausibility structures of the two poles. And we are not just talking about having a dialogue in our mind. The conversations may also be aloud in the open marketplace of ideas. Take, for example, the way that Jesus consistently argued with the prevailing plausibility structures of both ancient Palestine and the Roman Empire. The plausibility structure of the Kingdom of God rejected the nonsensical conservative legalism of the Pharisees as well as the idolatrous, liberal state worship of the Romans. Jesus even spoke about his method of argument with the reigning plausibility structures of his era by likening himself to a type of spiritual doctor who came for the sick.

Jesus' physician metaphor is a significant one. Perhaps we ought to view ourselves more in terms of being doctors rather than cultural warriors for either the Left or Right. Ours seems to be a task requiring much knowledge and practice as we are led by the Holy Spirit and not by the popular prognosticators of the day. But getting a doctorate in plausibility structures does not happen overnight. One must consider how to acquire great skill in studying the biblical drama which culminates in the revelation of Jesus Christ while, at the same time, becoming more and more fluent in the languages of powers and principalities at work in the world.

Arguing from a Kingdom of God perspective with those firmly entrenched in other plausibility structures may seem like a tremendous, if not impossible, challenge. When we refer to arguing, however, we are not talking about heated discourse which ends in tense stalemate or even violence. We are also not speaking of toleration in its current cultural usage. We refer to argument in the sense of vigorously honorable and admirable debate based on truth, complete with much inquiry and supportive points of departure in conversation. The Socratic Method seems to be a good fit for such argument. Consider, for instance, that the current cultural insistence upon a totally tolerant and inclusive society ironically hinders itself from achieving its ends. The telos of today's focus on tolerance appears to be some kind of idealistic society of humanists where debate is limited due to its supposedly offensive nature. The only arguments which are allowed are those which dare not offend the protectors of cultural unity.

Christian Realists could view this current popular form of tolerance as an abhorrent vice on true understanding, action, and basic freedom of speech and assembly. Christian Realism has few safe spaces, if any. In fact, without the tension that comes from argument, we would be hard pressed to achieve a kind of harmonious, informed relationships for which we seek. Put simply, everyone should have a right to be wrong, no matter how offended one may become.

To assess the plausibility structures of one's community requires cultural exegesis. Consider, for instance, the difficulty in finding the balance between the pole of the Kingdom of God and the pole of American conservatism/liberalism. One may find it difficult, if not impossible, to understand how their political bents are woven so tightly to the Kingdom of God. It is a tangled web that we weave, especially when it comes to Christianity in the United States. There seems to be no getting the conservative and liberal cats back into the proverbial bag once the Puritans and Separatists let them out. For example, consider the ways in which some churches prop up certain political candidates and ideologies as though the candidates were nearly equal to the first apostles. The cancers of evangelical nationalism and mainline denominational socialism can certainly deceive and devour those who have little to no experience investigating plausibility structures.

How do we untangle such a web? Perhaps we can think about those realities which transcend or even overshadow prevailing cultural logic. Such reality is true whether we like it or not. Since most social scientists would agree that culture is acquired socially and not biologically, we can surmise with great assurance that there are certain truths and aspects of such truths which remain true no matter the circumstance or culture.

Let's take the idea of success. American culture, on the whole, defines success from an empirical sense, meaning that a person's success is mostly tied to the amount one produces, acquires, or shares. In a biblical sense, success is defined in terms of one's reconciled relationship to God and to neighbor. For instance, Jesus explicitly said that "the first shall be last," and "The greatest among you shall be the servant," and "One must become like a child in order to inherit the Kingdom of God." Jesus himself lived a life that many, if not most, Americans today would consider dull and unsuccessful. He never ran for office, invented a technological gadget, made a name for himself as a content creator on media platforms, or used violence as a coercive tool over his followers. Yet, he paid the ransom for our sins.

If we take a leaf from the playbook of Jesus, we can find that success is neither dependent on political and social power nor monetary capital. Success appears contingent upon wisdom and following God. Our human finitude however brings us a kind of anxiety, which leads one to lie to the self and perhaps spend a lifetime trying to convince others to buy into his/her lie that success is just the product of sheer talent, good works, money saving ability, and the ability to get overcome one's competitors.[11] The lie about success can never quite seem to achieve a fully truthful status, however, since it is detached from reality. The culturally transcendent presupposition that success is found in following Jesus shows us the sheer folly of building bigger barns. Brunner says it thusly: "Christ crucifies the 'successful' man."[12]

Consequently, the plausibility structure of Christian Realists should be governed more by the culture-transcendent presuppositions which come to life in the Bible. In fact, we refer to culture-transcendent presuppositions by its more understandable name: consecrated common sense. This is why some Christian Realists may take a more skeptical or honest view of progress in our world. Wide eyed idealists can come at life from the reigning plausibility structure of their culture and attempt to make progress in terms of the culturally determined norms based on the anxious lies we are told.

For example, we supposedly make progress in terms of technology these days to bring the world together in harmony and love. It is a lie however that such harmony can be a human achievement. Such a lie is based on the fabrication of fact that we can overcome our anxiety and finitude to solve our most vexing problem—living

---

11. Niebuhr, *The Nature and Destiny*, 251–54.

12. Brunner, *The Divine Imperative*, 284.

together in peace. We may call this fabrication a lie since it both comes from a place of social anxiety and from our willingness to overstep the bounds placed on us by our Creator. In other words, this plausibility structure suggests that the only way we could achieve total love and harmony on earth in our own human will would be for us to become our own gods. Technology then becomes a tool in the lives of people who are utilizing their own bents towards self-deification to control others and coerce them into a forced harmony. Yet, why is it that, even though we have seemingly countless options for engaging in social media, we feel even lonelier than ever?

The culture-transcendent presupposition of the Christian Scripture is that we certainly cannot become gods. The temptation to do so is as old as Adam and Eve's encounter with the serpent in the Garden of Eden. Try as we may, we must temper our idealistic notions of achieving some sort of lasting peace between people due to our penchant towards seizing power over others for our own self-interests.

Are we saying then that we ought to live in some sort of hopeless, Luddite existence without progress, technological know-how, and efforts to overcome evil with good? No! It really depends on the type of progress to which you are referring. In a sense, life is easier when it comes to technology as compared to centuries ago, but we must remember that with technological progress comes newer problems. One may think particularly here of the economic, social, and political problems arising from the progress of artificial intelligence or the environmental problems borne out of the Industrial Revolution.

Shall we therefore reconsider our definition and view of progress? Perhaps. For instance, we may not look at progress as some sort of savior to world ills. Despite our constant progress, we still have not eliminated human evil. Progress therefore is and always will be tainted and limited by sin until the return of Christ.[13] Perhaps it is more worthwhile for us to think of progress as the ways in which we mature in loving God and neighbor. This maturing

13. Niebuhr, *The Nature and Destiny*, 24–25.

process works over time to glorify God through recognizing and then detaching from self-interest that we find in doing all sorts of work—even the best humanitarian efforts.

Yet we do not give up on work because of our human finitude. Quite the contrary! We embrace the challenge of our finitude through faith in Christ to crucify our flesh and relentless desire to fit into the successful idolatry of the American plausibility structure. Christians make progress when the cross becomes that which people see in our work more than they see us.

The second tier of living life from a more macro-evangelistic level is to recognize and deal with confirmation bias. Confirmation bias is a term used to describe our penchant to seek out, utilize, or even manipulate information to support our beliefs, narratives, and ends. While some may think this term is rather new, there is evidence suggesting that Pythagoras coined the idea of confirmation bias in the 6th century BC. The idea of confirmation bias is ultimately rooted in self-interest and one-upmanship. We see it vividly play out on social media when people pass along links to news articles or other information in attempts to justify their dissenting opinions on reality.

But what's the difference between confirmation bias and just good, old-fashioned factual debate? Much of the difference lies in the will of one who attempts to win an argument at all costs. For example, doctoral seminary students often do both quantitative and qualitative research for a culminating project to earn their degree. They are to state their biases up-front but allow the researched information either to confirm or deny their biases. In other words, true researchers and seekers understand that they have biases towards all sorts of data. Human beings cannot help but to be biased. Yet, we are to state these biases and allow room for correction. Honest debate should result in learning and correction for people of different biases and outlooks. Hardly any correction is possible for those stuck in the cycle of confirmation bias. It's as if one is wearing blinders to ward off any influences from potentially disagreeable information or people.

Legalists and relativists over the years seemed to have dealt with confirmation bias through a variety of ways, most of which may be generally ineffective. Brunner outlines three common but faulty approaches to what we call confirmation bias.[14] First, there is a positivist approach that tends to ignore or even remove the biases of the individual from the empirical data collected in community. That is, it should not matter what the biases are of the individual. Only straight facts should count. This approach ignores the environment in which both the individual and community function and assumes that truth cannot be tested. Faith is totally removed from the positivist equation.

Second, the idealistic approach suggests that individuals have biases but can transcend such biases to find commonality with the other. This approach relativizes truth to such a degree that no one is really right or wrong about particular issues. Understanding and dialogue become the supreme virtues of this approach and vastly outweigh verifiable facts and necessary tension.

Third, the romantic approach advocates for the rejection of traditions which fail to serve the ends of a majority group in power. The individual and his/her biases are essentially said to be outdated or superstitious before the ultimate desires of the communal group. Truthful, yet inconvenient, information may be labeled as dangerous. Think book burning. What matters for the romantic is that creativity and higher order thinking be allowed to flourish for the supposed good of all. The politics which emerge from this approach could be characterized as being more "for the people," rather than "by the people."

A Christian approach to confirmation bias stands mostly in opposition to the other three views just described. While we are not to rely solely on empirical data, we are neither to relativize truth nor detach ourselves from the supposed superstitiousness of Christian tradition for the greater good. Perhaps the Apostle Paul most adequately characterized the Christian approach to confirmation bias when he advocated for what he termed the ministry of reconciliation. He recognized that the best way to achieve our ends as believers involves restoration of relationships through the Holy Spirit-led ministry of Jesus through us.

14. Brunner, *The Divine Imperative*, 297–307.

Yet, human beings are incapable of overcoming biases and presenting a good Christian witness all on our own. Christians therefore argue and defend the truth from a standpoint of having the right to be wrong. In other words, our faith in Christ and his restorative work in our lives is that which gives our arguments and belief system credence in the marketplace of ideas. Ours is not to win an argument based on our biases and empirical data, but it is to reconcile in our relationships with others as Christ has reconciled us to himself. The church accordingly is to function as the environment in which reconciled relationships in Christ are modeled effectively to the outside world. The church is to be in the world but not of it. She can do this through the power of Christ's reconciling ministry among us.

But how do we go about the ministry of reconciliation among people with vastly different ideas and even among those who would utilize coercion, manipulation, and even violence to silence us? Consider the following quotation from William Sloan Coffin, who uniquely summarizes Brunner's arguments.

> [There] are those who prefer certainty to truth, those in church who put the purity of dogma ahead of the integrity of love. And what a distortion of the gospel it is to have limited sympathies and unlimited certainties, when the very reverse, to have limited certainties but unlimited sympathies, is not only more tolerant but far more Christian. For "who has known the mind of God?" [Romans 11:34] And didn't Paul also insist that if we fail in love we fail in all other things?[15]

Coffin's quote seems rightly to argue that purity of dogma (unlimited certainties) must take second place to the integrity of love (unlimited sympathies) in the Christian experience. Coffin not only echoes the theological praxis of Brunner, suggesting that Christians can never quite arrive at a "dead center" between the poles of traditionalism and anti-traditionalism. When we boil that down, we find that Christianity is an exercise in what famed musician Bob Seger called running against the wind. We move between what to leave in

---

15. Coffin, "Liberty," 106–7.

and what to leave out. Christianity is therefore a both-and, not an either-or. Any error should be made on the side of unlimited sympathies since we are too finite to achieve the impossible possibility of Christ's law of love.

But what about our certainties? Surely Christianity cannot be reduced to a few relativized doctrines. We begin by noting a few points in the New Testament at which certainty is discussed relative to agape. In Romans 8:38, Paul advocated for certainty when it comes to our complete acceptance by God through faith in Jesus Christ. Similarly, in Philippians 1:6, Paul argued doggedly for certainty in God's ability to keep one's salvation from being corrupted. The writer of Hebrews also jumped on the certainty bandwagon by declaring faith as that which involves surety in the unseen.

Consider however how these writers' certainties highlighted the ministerial over the magisterial. We can make a strong argument that their brand of certainty came not from their ability to give mental assent to theological postulates but from their search to add understanding to their faith in Christ. As we have learned from Tillich, faith is both the courageous act and attitude which accepts the inherent risk of putting all one's eggs in God's basket. Equating faith in Christ with total certainty beyond all doubt is therefore not biblical faith at all. Unlimited certainty is a type of faith for sure, but it is that which is ultimately concerned about moral performance and perfection in lieu of a cross, and thus it is an idolatrous faith.

Yet, those who ardently defend Coffin's "unlimited sympathies" should assess carefully how and who they criticize. A healthy dose of realism tempers our capacity to lash out at the intolerant. In fact, there may be nothing more hypocritical today than Christians who cannot tolerate the intolerant. The absolutizing of relativism may be the final undoing of many once powerfully effective Christian congregations. At the end of the day, a loving yet courageous faith commits to living between the poles of revelation given and revelation anticipated.

Perhaps the best lesson in this approach comes from the distraught father in the Gospel of Mark who exclaimed, "Lord, I believe! Help my unbelief!"

What we are talking about, in a nutshell, is how the ministry of reconciliation essentially means that we live out our radically monotheistic faith in Christ by becoming less polarized. Our faith, expressed through agape love, does its best to hear and see things from another's point of view without becoming either relativized or dogmatic. It is a tempered, middle way that values both the uniqueness of the individual and the necessity of the community while still remaining critical of the pitfalls of hyper-individualism and group think run amok.

According to Brunner such a way of life begins with embracing the life of the one(s) with whom we communicate as "my life,"[16] meaning that we approach another from the standpoint of, "If I were in his/her shoes, then what would I do or advise?" This concept is as basic as Jesus' Golden Rule. Consider also, for instance, the ancient book of Job. After Job experienced such horrendous losses, his three friends—even though they seemed to have good intentions—leaned more towards the pole of hyper-individuality in their dealings with Job. Offering dogmatic and legalistic axioms to Job did little to soothe his physical and emotional wounds, if at all. It turns out that the friends' initial action of simply sitting in silence with Job may have been one the most loving and balanced, radically monotheistic things they could have done instead of shooting off their mouths. Sometimes a realist simply needs to acknowledge what is by providing the least amount of commentary possible.

As we live out such a balanced approach, it becomes clearer that our neighbors are those whom we serve. They are not the ones who reside in our echo chamber nor pundits who bully others in the name of Christian conquest. They are ones to whom we go as ambassadors for a greater kingdom which is not of this world.

But what about those who are genuinely wrong, offend us, or simply get on our nerves? When trying to live in the balance between revelation given and revelation anticipated, Christian Realists advise that hostility may be used, but only in the way of Christ. Jesus appeared to be hostile towards specific groups of people, most notably the religious legalists of his day and governmental

16. Brunner, *The Divine Imperative*, 322.

authorities who abused others for their own power. Can we not say that Jesus' display of anger in the Temple was anything but hostile? We can even describe the Judgment to come as hostile. Jesus' description of the Judgment as a separation of sheep from goats is particularly bone chilling. Yet, our Lord's hostility was "tempered by a grateful acceptance of human life, coupled with a readiness to serve."[17] Can the same be said of us?

In the final analysis, the two-tiered system of macro-evangelism and political involvement of Christian Realism described above may prove more helpful than the polarized conservative-liberal options. Its approach simply refrains from codifying certain rules or laws of conduct while allowing room for maneuvering between revelation given and revelation to come. From this standpoint, the Christian Realist may be in a uniquely helpful position to offer more suggestions to both polarized sides in conflict since he/she concentrates more on what is in terms of culturally transcendent propositions, plausibility structures, and confirmation bias. We therefore stand ready to offer solutions and suggestions through the lens of consecrated common sense rather than through faulty, Pharisaical logic or through progressive, unrealistic ideology.

The next question which concerns us involves how we put feet to the fire of Christian Realism. We ought to explore how such realism works in the context of everyday life and events, especially within those problems that arise with few easy answers in the context of both the local church and the wider community of neighbors. It is hoped that the applications which follow begin to steer us away from the conservative/liberal divide and towards a more balanced, radical monotheism.

---

17. Brunner, *The Divine Imperative*, 338.

4

Putting the Balanced Approach to Work

The radically monotheistic Balanced Approach of Christian Realism may be in applied in virtually any number of settings and contexts. Particular attention shall be given here to ways we may apply the Balanced Approach to local church life and to the current volatile political climate of the United States. In so doing, we will attempt to provide encouraging groundwork for following God's call by faith.

A quick word about faith is in order before we dive fully into talk of applying Christian Realism in its Balanced Approach. We have already defined faith as the state of being ultimately concerned. For the Christian, our ultimate concern is to be directed towards God. As such, faith expresses itself in both action and love, with agape love for the Lord and our neighbors being the most appropriate way, biblically speaking, to act according to our ultimate concern.

Christian Realism causes us to reconsider whether our faith is genuine, or more specifically how disingenuous our faith may be in any given context. For instance, some people may claim to be Christ-followers, and yet their ultimate concern has become diluted or even idolatrous. But how can one tell the extent to which their faith as ultimate concern for God has turned into a henotheistic type of belief system?

An investigation to root out idolatrous elements of faith within ourselves begins with recognizing the constant allure of polytheistic gods such as one's nation or material success. Such gods often use fanciful propaganda and produce a seemingly strong leader or administration who promises human fulfillment on a large scale. Tillich warns us, however, that such a faith collapses over time and leads to chaos since people and materials can give us no sense of ultimacy for long.[1]

We can also be alert to the ways in which our ultimate concern affects our behavior towards other people. As we have seen in our examination of fundamentalism and humanism, we can sometimes separate our faith from love by codifying ultimate concern into legalistic expressions or manipulating it into a kind of self-indulgent mysticism.[2] Christian Realism invites us to temper the codification of religious rules and the human-centered mysticism to let love root into our faith further in and deeper down. When we reduce agape love down either to a series of doctrinal legal codes or to a conflagration of emotions, we have missed the boat of what it means to be ultimately concerned in the way of Jesus.

Which gets us back to the idea about living in the tension between both subjective and objective poles of the Christian faith. The subjective pole is that which is characterized by one's fervency and emotive passion for Christ while the objective pole deals with the more deontological, or duty-bound, elements of faith in action.[3] Finding the better balance perhaps occurs best when one moves away from placing so much trust in human rationalism either to build an ideal ecclesial community or to become a lone ranger type.[4] When we begin to live in the tension between the subjective and objective aspects of ultimate concern for God through

1. Tillich, *The Essential Tillich*, 110
2. Tillich, *The Essential Tillich*, 113.
3. Tillich, *The Essential Tillich*, 109
4. Tillich, *The Essential Tillich*, 116–17.

the leadership of Jesus Christ in the Holy Spirit, then we are much better equipped to add tremendous value to the local church and wider community of neighbors. Let's examine, then, how this kind of action can take place.

The Balanced Approach and The Local Church

Christian Realists tend to accept the church as she is, warts and all. It could be easy however for realism to turn into skepticism. Given the polarities of fundamentalism and humanism at work in local churches, Christian Realists can apply the Balanced Approach to faith and make a lasting difference for the Lord in a number of ways.

A good starting place may be how Christian Realists can assist churches to become less distracted by secularization in their surrounding contexts. Secularization is an expression of idolatrous faith that occurs when one gives more energy and resources over to interests outside of the koinonia, or Spirit-led fellowship of the church body. For instance, when we drop out of church and dedicate our Sundays to team sports, we could say that we have become too secularized. Yet, churches on both the Right and the Left have pointed their fingers with judgmentalism at those who have been deemed as too secular. Some churches and pastors even consistently preach against certain activities that are too worldly to be acceptable among good church people.

With all the finger pointing, many churches make the grave mistake of calling out the sins of others instead of looking at their own failures. People in churches would do much better to understand just how imperfect they are, not so they can get away with more sin, but so they can welcome those who are more secularized and work together on the deeper, ultimate issues and problems that we all face. Cooperation concerning ultimate problems from a perspective of faith in Jesus Christ alongside others is actualized in the previously discussed ministry of reconciliation. Reconciliation chiefly occurs when we realize that God is with us and has revealed himself perfectly to us in Jesus Christ, and therefore we repent and worship only God. In fact, secularization at its core is simply a fancy title for those activities we do as an attempt to become our own gods, or self-deification. When we choose to follow our own paths or become our own deities, we become more inclined to use anything at our disposal to control and rule over others.

We are therefore saying that the church is not a collective of people who are no longer secular heathen and are opposed to the masses of sinful degenerates out there. The church is an institution constructed by God—not for judgment but for service. The church can never be some idealistic shrine to those legalists or humanists who are better than anyone else. Rather, the church is to be a hospital for sinners. Jesus is less concerned about finger-pointing and more with rescuing people who are deeply hurting. We can join Jesus in this mission of hope as a church as we relinquish our desire for self-deification and watch out for how secularism is affecting us. This relinquishment is an obvious form of balancing the objective and subjective poles of faith as ultimate concern for Christ.

Yet, too many churches and pastors seem caught up in their own significance rather than reflecting the significance of Jesus Christ. In fact, Christian Realism posits that we must beware of churches that stake their all on how good their people are or how wonderful the pastor is. Personality-driven churches can easily devolve into a cult based on the self-deification of one leader or leadership group. Churches that operate on gimmicky, attractional events just to get more people in the door appear to show their true colors, as well. They seem more concerned with the quantity of people than with the quality. Jesus told us to make disciples of his narrow way, not students of the latest popular religious fad. Christian Realism consequently notes the irony of those churches who, although they act either according to rigid rules or overly humanistic emotions, claim to have escaped secularization when it is they themselves who illustrate the very meaning of secularization.

Consequently, we ask, "What is the true purpose of the local church?" For Christian Realists, the concept of a so-called Purpose Driven church is not all that appealing. We offer no blueprint or design for programming adaptation at a local church level. Due to the nature of reality in our time, Christian Realism suggests that a church must do more than simply make ancient concepts and principles relevant for modern Americans. It rather advocates for churches to wrestle more with problems in their community than adapt purposes for a select few who have enough money to pay a pastor and keep the church's bills paid. We feel that the questions being asked by the wider public are those deserving of deeper theological reflection and even increased tension. The realistic church should neither shy away from tension nor embrace the cult of tolerance. Tolerance may bring less tension, but it also negates debate and free exchange of ideas, an exchange which becomes crucial if people are to discern *what is*.

Accordingly, Christian Realism at work in a local church looks much less like those congregations given over to overtly consumeristic marketplace tactics so common among secular businesses in America. Struggling with the more crucial and deeper aspects of life simply cannot take place if one shops for spiritual and religious goods from a church in the same way one would shop for groceries at a store or on Amazon. The realist Christian life is not one based on some sort of church marketplace, or data analytics which reveal what church has the greatest amount of spiritual goods or the best pastoral staff that can cater to one's whims. When Christian Realism becomes firmly rooted in a local congregation, that community of faith may even find itself on the outside looking in. The church may not have the most members or the biggest budget to support consumeristic, purpose-driven programming.

Christian Realists thus also advocate for the church to have one, central purpose: to increase the love of God and the love of neighbor. While this purpose may sound too simplistic to some, we find it to be the most practical and biblical. All of church life may be organized around this purpose, as well. Yet, how may we define the term "love" so we may live more effectively on purpose for the Lord? The biblical definition of the type of love to which we refer here comes from the Koine Greek word *agape*, having to do with a sacrificial and humble service of another. It is a rugged type of love that gives all for a central cause. It is thus the best expression of one's ultimate concern, or faith in Jesus Christ.

That being said, we must pause at this point and share what agape love is not. For instance, love for God and neighbor is not necessarily passive or unemotive due to its rugged nature. Can we not suggest that Jesus' outburst in the Temple was a rather violent but nevertheless appropriate expression of love? He protected vital interests of the Kingdom—namely prayer and the deterrence of stealing from poor/widows—by overturning tables and cracking a whip on the money changers. The idea that love must be somewhat disconnected from any expression of power is nonsensical from a realistic point of view. A touchy-feely type of love may work for a romantic comedy, but such fallacy is ultimately a make-believe expression of rugged love for God and neighbor.

Due to its intimate connection to faith as the state of being ultimately concerned about God, agape love will assert itself and become courageous for the kingdom. In fact, we could say that true agape love will know how to work without a net, so to speak. It takes the risk of plummeting to its demise so that the Lord may be uplifted. Yet, we must also understand that agape love is not a form of unchecked brute force. Fanatical expressions of love for neighbor can and often do lead to idolatry. Think Christian nationalism. So, we advocate here for both the subjective passion of faith and objective courage of worshipful action to be united and balanced in agape love for God and neighbor.

Agape love may be expressed in a multiplicity of ways in a local church which rallies around the one unifying purpose which has been revealed and lived out perfectly through the incarnation and life of Jesus Christ. Most notably, agape love is manifested by our utilizing what Martin Buber called the "I-Thou" relationship. An I-Thou model of interacting with one another is favorable than an I-It situation in which one view another as more of an object than a uniquely thinking and complex subject. The I-It relationship is simply one of transaction, where the other becomes a means to our ends. Fidelity in relationship cannot exist in an I-It situation.

However, it should be noted that the I-Thou model of relating to others is accomplished effectively only when we acknowledge the other as a free-thinking self.[5] The other is capable of just as much fidelity or infidelity as we are, and their choices should not

---

5. Niebuhr, *Faith on Earth*, 50.

be the result of any type of coercion on our part. In fact, H. Richard Niebuhr invites us to consider an I-Thou relationship in a triadic way, meaning that there ought to be three components to the relationship. We normally view relationships in terms of dyad in which we have (1) the I and Thou (me and you) which exists and (2) the faith or trust relationship between the I and Thou which makes conversation possible.[6] In other words, in a healthy relationship we both acknowledge the personhood and existence of the other, and then we create an environment of fidelity by learning to trust one another which leads to in kind reciprocity. In an unhealthy relationship, the reciprocal actions turns treasonous.

Niebuhr suggests we add a third component, a common cause or object.[7] The common object binds the I-Thou to a trusting, healthy relationship of fidelity. But what is the common object? In realistic Christian communities, the common object is truth, or simply what is reality. We could even name the common object "Truth" as it is located perfectly in Jesus Christ. The Truth is something that is more important than simply a cause that binds people together in fidelity-driven relationships. Truth is also that which serves a larger purpose than nationalism, crony capitalism, communism, or even debates about sexual identity.[8] In fact, Niebuhr rightly proposes that the healthiest I-Thou relationships built on Truth are "communities," while those built on lesser important common causes should be called "associations."[9]

We hear much today from people who are searching for authentic communities, but do they understand the difference between communities and associations? Niebuhr defines associations as "organizations of interests rather than of men, for each individual in the association tends to function in that setting as an interest or set of interests rather than as a whole man."[10] Communities, rather, are distinctive in that they are organized around people themselves

---

6. Niebuhr, *Faith on Earth*, 47.

7. Niebuhr, *Faith on Earth*, 51.

8. Niebuhr, *Faith on Earth*, 52.

9. Niebuhr, *Faith on Earth*, 54–58.

10. Niebuhr, *Faith on Earth*, 54–55.

instead of interests. In fact, we could say that communities have more internalized relationships as opposed to associations which would be more externally focused.[11] In other words, associations concern themselves more with things while communities focus on people.

Keep in mind, as well, that there is a rather simple way for discerning whether a community is becoming an association. If a community begins to mistake covenants for contracts for the sake of limited ends, then an association is blooming.[12] Yet, a community stands strong when its participants remain so focused on a common object that, even when conflict arises, they remain diligently committed to their fidelity for one another.[13]

But how does such a covenanted community function pragmatically in the context of a local church? Let's start with a few observations about the pastoral office within a church community. Christian Realists notice the obvious creep of a more humanistic faith into the pastoral office and subsequently prescribed leadership styles, namely the notion that an alpha-male pastor directs the activities of a church as a business manager or CEO to meet monetary and growth obligations under the guise of serving others. What we mean by "humanist" in this context is that system in which a church shifts its ultimate concern away from God and toward personal fulfillment for its client base. The pastor of the humanist system essentially becomes one who must empower others to do ministry in order to meet the church's bottom line of people pleasing, while he himself stands rather aloof from boots-on-the-ground action.

Is there an off-ramp for pastors to journey into a more biblical, priestly, and prophetic office? Realistically, finding an off-ramp from the humanistic expressway is an almost untenable exercise since humanism's philosophies have become so engrained among contemporary American Protestants on both the Right and the Left. A good starting point however for designing such an off-ramp

11. Niebuhr, *Faith on Earth*, 54.

12. Niebuhr, *Faith on Earth*, 57.

13. Niebuhr, *Faith on Earth*, 58.

would be the proliferation of self-criticism in churches.[14] Self-criticism in this sense refers to one's ability to laugh at themselves or to discover one's finiteness in the larger picture of the kingdom of God in order to defer one's will to that of the Holy Spirit.

It is healthy for pastors to help churches take assessments about those things which deserve both serious and humorous criticism. Such assessments would have to be designed at the local church level since these churches are seemingly more familiar with their own contexts than anyone else. Yet, a willingness to theologically examine the wheels and the gears of a church's daily ministry takes courage as well as the ability to discern one's calling. It is precisely at this point that a pastor may do some of his or her best work.

We may liken culturally appropriate, self-critical assessments in the church to prescription medications—ones that provide potent antidotes to disease and inflammation in the Body of Christ. These prescriptions have various helpful components, the primary ingredient being a trust in God which overcomes the virus of natural religion in a church. If a pastor inoculates his/her flock to natural religion, then that church will be able to develop and maintain a healthy focus on the Great Commission.

Both conservative and liberal churches also struggle mightily with natural religion. Natural religion is the tendency in all people to mistake reality as the creation of One who is an enemy—that if life is like this, then the God who created it must be our enemy. The one who is infected by natural religion takes a stand of mistrust against either God, a higher power, or that which is considered to be transcendent. Even Christians can bend to the will of natural religion when they face seemingly impossible or traumatic circumstance or cave to certain kinds of sin. Some may even victimize themselves in the face of challenges, which leads to the mixing of self-help, New Ageism with Christian theology.

In more fundamentalist or legalistic congregations, natural religion usually results in a kind of henotheism in which God is said to require absolute appeasement through the means of what

---

14. Tillich, *The Essential Tillich*, 125.

Niebuhr calls "rituals of placation."[15] These rituals could be anything from paying certain penances to public shaming. It views God as a hard taskmaster. Pastors of natural religion often solidify the distrust of God in a congregation to the extent of wielding abusive power under the banner of "doing what is best for the welfare of the group." He may use threats, coercive tactics, and forbid his flock from certain taboo activities or voting for certain politicians which would cause the Lord to unleash disaster at any moment. And when disaster strikes, you can be sure that the church would discuss things like, "Who caused this man's blindness? His parents or he himself?"

More liberal or humanistic churches also flirt heavily with what is sometimes called natural religion. It often comes out in a congregation's anxiety or fear that they are up against one who is primarily responsible for preventing them from becoming their best selves or living their best life. Due to this seemingly irresolvable anxiety, naturally religious humanists may resort to constructing an alternative reality in which they mistakenly believe that God simply exists for one's pleasure. Evil is thusly discounted as something of a transitory nature which will be shortly cast away due to human progress, and a pleasurable kind of Epicureanism is supported through all kinds of exegetical and biblical gymnastics. Pride and sensuality are disguised as religiously appropriate and tactful in the presence of a rather unknowable God, the wrath of whom we must avoid at all costs by allowing ourselves to believe the lie of the serpent in the Garden that we can become our own gods and finally defeat the One who is transcendent over this shabby reality we call life.

How then can our trust in God overcome such a vicious virus like natural religion? We want to shy away from cynicism at this point. Jesus promised that the gates of hell will not prevail against his church. Yet pastors should make their congregations aware of natural religion and yank it up by the root. When people become more critically aware of their foibles and concretely understand that all have sinned, natural religion begins to leave the body. In fact,

15. Niebuhr, *Faith on Earth*, 74.

pastors can make tremendous progress in congregations steeped in natural religion through helping their flocks begin to re-trust God. Since we are so finite, we cannot see very well into the depths of God. We therefore should not allow ourselves to give in to the anxiety and mistrust caused by our finiteness. No amount of appeasement nor escape into Epicureanism will satiate the deep longings of the soul for long.

We must encourage one another about the God who is Emmanuel, or "God With Us." The only one who can situate our trust and anxiety correctly and effectively is Jesus Christ. Consequently, churches must be equipped to turn loose of me-centered faith and focus on Christ—not as an Object, but as the Primary Subject of life. As the planets revolve around the sun, so we must revolve around Christ. He is a Person to be trusted, not a coagulation of propositions into which we must buy, appease, or escape.[16] Let it be said again that the church and the Christian life is not to be purpose driven but Person driven.

What we are essentially talking about here is the responsibility among pastors and church leaders to help people reconstruct their faith in Jesus Christ instead of deconstructing it due to their anxieties. Christian realism accordingly asserts that a church's theology should not be either an individualistic or merely a private affair to be kept within the walls of a congregational meeting spot. It is to be done in a community whose common object is the Truth as revealed in Jesus Christ, not an association built on interests. If God is the Person to be trusted, then that trust would result in loving, thoughtful action to our neighbors.

Christian Realists can refer to a church's communal public exercise of theology as "practical theology," or praxis. Simply put, practical Christian theology may be defined as faith in Christ seeking understanding. It is usually characterized by a robust evangelistic witness, biblically based congregational worship, conflict resolution, and gospel proclamation in the way of Jesus. In fact, the practical theology of Christian Realism among may be more strategically situated than other legalistic or humanistic belief systems to have a maximum impact for the Kingdom of God in today's marketplace of ideas. We therefore now turn our attention to the demonstration of a realistic practical Christian theology outside the walls of church buildings.

The Balanced Approach and Public Expressions of Christian Realism

Why would a practical expression of Christian Realism make a marked difference beyond the walls of church buildings in American culture today? Much of the effect would have to do with the overall sense of disillusionment in contemporary society. We define disillusionment primarily as a negative attitude based upon one's disappointments in both culture and fellow people. Disillusionment is the result of being let down consistently after putting high hopes in something or someone. More specifically, many Christian pastors, theologians, and ex-church goers have experienced great disappointments because they have replaced a trust in God with a trust in people. When others let them down, they become disillusioned—some almost to a point of despondency. Yet some people try to salvage any sort of hope by not only rejecting the church but also embracing a kind of spiritual humanitarianism that does not trust in God or man, per se, yet it trusts in some sort of principle or law that progress is inevitable. The mantra goes: "If we're just good humans, then it will all work out somehow in the end."

We can unfortunately place some of the blame for this disillusionment at the feet of some Christians and churches in America. Promised yet empty reforms and the church's promotion of social enterprises of both the Right and the Left have alienated not a few. Consider for instance how American churches of all denominational stripes and political bents defend nationalism, war, poverty, sexual immorality, and the like. It can appear that churches today tend to be mouthpieces for the two major political parties in America rather than outposts for the Kingdom of God.

To better deal with this sense of disillusionment, Christian Realism presents both a critical and practical theology in its Balanced

Approach. Let's examine then how Christian Realism can help believers in their witness to and engagement with surrounding culture.

Because it holds both fundamentalism and humanism in tension, Christian Realism offers us a unique perspective on how believers may engage in political conversations and practice their theology within the public sphere. Rather than embrace either the Right or the Left, Christian Realists would rather attempt to temper political idealism while also helping and encouraging those who have been disillusioned or even abused by the corrupted power systems of conservatives and liberals. At this point, we may be pressed to inquire about the political system which would be most conducive to effective Christian practice. If we knew the best system, then we could take correct action, or so the thinking goes. Yet, while critical theological examination of any political system is always in order, it is not necessarily the first or primary way of expressing Christian Realism in the public arena. The primary lens through which we look at taking our first steps of public Christian Realism is that of Jesus Christ.

Consider, for instance, that Jesus seemed rather indifferent to the political systems of his day.[17] We could even suggest that Jesus, although highly critical of the Roman political system, accepted it as it was. That is, Jesus wasn't going to use the government as a means for his ends. Neither was he interested in any sort of governmental overthrow or revolution. The Roman official, Pontius Pilate, obviously recognized Jesus' lack of substantive, worldly political interest when he found the Lord to have broken no Imperial laws. Pilate simply wanted to rough Jesus up a bit and let him go. Pilate even seemed somewhat aghast that the religious leaders would dare call for Jesus' head.

We may assert therefore that, no matter the political system under which Christians find themselves, their primary allegiance is to God's Kingdom first. This allegiance will have public ramifications, but it will also understand that God reigns in spite of anything that communism, socialism, monarchy, or democracy can throw at Him. Should we not be more realistic to inquire how we can seek

17. Diefenthaler, *Paradox*, 143.

first God's Kingdom rather than seek first how whatever political system we prefer can be manipulated to become God's Kingdom? Ours is to obey God rather than men anyway.

But does this mean that Christians should withdraw from the most part from political or governmental service? May it never be! Withdrawing from the public sphere only hinders rather than helps churches and Christians to reignite their witness and passion for faith and evangelism. In fact, Christian Realists assert that there is a certain amount of accommodation that the church must make to the world and its way of doing things to insure we find enough common ground with others for effective gospel sharing and disciple making. In fact, when we find common points of conversation in public, Christians have the advantage of sharing the biblical revelation in ways that could do more for the ministry of reconciliation than any other political system.

How then Shall We Live? Responding Realistically to the Contemporary Tension between Communism and Democracy

The two most popular political and economic systems of our day are still communism/socialism and democracy. Christians have tended to absolutize either system for their moral goals and ends. For instance, liberal Christians appear to have become more comfortable with communism, while conservative fundamentalists opt for their brand of democracy. But why? The links between these groups and systems have been explored above, but in a nutshell, we could argue that the majority of middle and upper class American Christians have thought less critically about how to apply their theology and more in terms of making religion less offensive. Liberals would especially seem keen on placing less emphasis on the tough nature of sin, while fundamentalists err on the side of preaching conversion without discipleship. Accordingly, a social gospel lends itself well to the trappings of communism, while the individualistic gospel of fundamentalists responds well to the democratic tendency to see who can shout the loudest and get their own way in the majority.

Let's explore then a way that Christian Realism assesses the systems of both communism and democracy. We will then put forward a number of proposals for Christian Realists as well as doctrines for effective and more realistic political involvement for Christians who want to escape from the chains of fundamentalism and/or liberalism in order to live in a better, more biblical tension between the two.

We begin our assessment by observing the utilitarian nature of both communism and democracy in our world today.[18] Utilitarianism is a that philosophy which seeks to promote the greatest happiness for the greatest number of people. Whatever the majority desires to be right is accordingly utilitarian. Both communists and democrats have long desired to control Christians to transform our worship to suit their purposes. And why have we gone along with them? It most likely has something to do with the fact that we get too easily caught up in groupthink. A politician from either the Right or Left says something that tickles our ears in ways that get us stirred up to support him/her and their cause. Little do we know that our worship is being manipulated for political ends.

Also, believers may not know the biblical narrative effectively enough to see the holes in the arguments of those supporting the prevailing political systems. Opposition to those in the majority of power may even be viewed as biblical heresy. From the perspective of Christian Realism, we are called to be repentant people who seek first the Kingdom of God. We are to repent of our sin not so that we may be a better communist or better democrat but because our minds and hearts have been changed by the grace of God. Faith is not to be viewed as blind but as seeing life as what is. When we walk by a blind faith, it is easier for us to be manipulated by those who want to use us as means to their ends.

With this in mind, let's dive deeper into analyzing and thus responding to these systems from a perspective of Christian Realism. A good starting point for our response is the biblical revelation to us concerning the image of God. We've emphatically stated in this volume the Christian Realist view that every person is created

18. Diefenthaler, *Paradox*, 364.

in the image of God and therefore is due dignity, value, and human rights. While this view somewhat aligns with both communist and democratic doctrines, we can assert that communism seems to fail more than democracy or capitalism to define or account rightly for the inequalities between people.

While every human being in the image of God is created equal, Christian Realists recognize that each human is different in terms of their function and responsibility. Keep in mind Paul's admonishment to the Corinthian believers that the church is one body but many parts. We are therefore equal in form but not in function. For example, a person with little to no skill at playing basketball should not have the same right as LeBron James to play on an NBA team. Everyone is created equal, but not everyone can be a professional athlete. This is reality in terms of our human essence and existence. Remember that a crow cannot become a fence. Yet, communism appears to aim for equality of both from and function, much like one would cut all trees in a forest to the same height in order to prevent the naturally taller trees from growing.

But why would communism aim for equality of function? Much of it has to do with communism's Marxist roots. In fact, we define communism here as more of an umbrella term that may be more akin to the goals of democratic socialism in the United States today, or the public ownership of the means of production. Consequently, Marxism can be a bit difficult to capture in a concise manner, but the philosophy basically comes out of Hegelian theology, which posits God as some sort of a cosmic clockmaker who wound up creation and left humankind to their own devices. Hegel asserted however that humanity is always making progress and that sin itself may even be a positive mechanism of progress for humanity.

Hegel's assertions, along with his concern for the group over the individual, laid significant groundwork for people like Marx to consider those powers and issues that supposedly impede human progress for the greatest good. One of the main issues impeding progress in Marx's mind had to do with economic determinism, or the idea that materialism is one of the main drivers in unequal societal relationships. This was to blame for so much poverty and the widening gap between the haves and the have-nots. In this line of thought, economic determinism has made for the inequality of people in both function and form. So, if we could steer economic determinism in our favor, then we could have a classless society of all equals. Such a society could only come about, however, with the overthrow of capitalism through revolution and the building of a state government which could control affairs of the people until a truly classless society finally emerges. Once a classless society was implemented, then there would no longer be the need for a state, much less an authoritarian one.[19]

The main goal of Marxism appears to be a stateless, classless society in which profits of business leaders (the bourgeois) are no longer seemingly robbed from the workers (the proletariat). This goal may be achieved when primarily wealthy, progressive people on the Left seize their opportunities to elevate the equality of function in their society at the local, state, and federal level. Support is especially strengthened for the Marxist cause through relegating freedom of speech or controlling narratives to tamp down the opinions of those who are not enlightened or progressive enough. Opponents may be de-platformed or deemed dangerous for saying unagreeable things as foes of socialism. Speech that strengthens the equality of function in the social order however is allowable and highly encouraged.[20]

On a practical level, Marxism is seemingly applied most effectively when the bourgeois associated with the Left in a given society helps the proletariat gain power through, ironically, democratic means. By democratic in this case, however, we mean government "for the people" instead of "by the people." Once the proletariat take the reigns of the society, then they are to bring about the goal of a classless state where everyone is equal in function until that state reaches a point of being totally free from any sort of political control. Yet, a cursory glimpse at the history of states based in Marxist ideology reveals that the power and control of the state only grows over time instead of diminishing.

19. Maston, *World Issues*, 152–55.
20. Maston, *World Issues*, 166–67.

Perhaps the most important thing we can say about Marxism from a perspective of Christian Realism is that a state built on pitting the bourgeois against the proletariat is one with a foundation of animosity instead of love. Hatred for others based primarily on economics seems to be one of the main strands of DNA in Marxist philosophy and pragmatism. As such, Christian Realists are better off rejecting such a program. Surely there are other, more effective ways to discuss and find agreement on economic issues other than by advocating for equality of function and taking over control of a state. Besides, we have already discussed how the oppressed have the tendency to take on the exact characteristic of their oppressors once they arrive in power.

Can we not also conclude that, from the point of view of Christian Realism, values materials more than people? If the individual is reduced to equality of function, then that individual can never rise above being a mere pawn in the grand scheme of a state-controlled society. For a philosophy like Marxism to claim that humanity can be perfected, it certainly seems paradoxically bent on reducing the dignity of individuals, if not bent on removing the sacredness of humans made in the image of God altogether.

Christian Realists seemingly have no other viable choice but to rid themselves of the scourge of Marxism in order to promote not only equality of form but also the reconciliation of people to both their neighbors and to God without much interference from the state, if any.

But how? A fresh focus on dignity of the individual seems in order. We are not cogs in a communistic wheel. We are sinners in need of grace. Living in the tension between our dignity as human beings and our dependence on God becomes paramount at this point.

Living in this tension brings us face-to-face with economic issues. Both communism and capitalism have powerful economic interests at their core. For the sake of argument, however, let's keep a discussion about economics simple, without being simplistic. For instance, can we rightly say as Christian Realists that the purpose of life is loving God with heart, soul, mind, and strength as well as loving our neighbor as ourselves? If this is the true north of the Christian's heart and attitude, then we will more effectively understand what economic system—even though flawed because of fallen humanity—presents the best way of meeting our responsibilities to God and neighbor. Maston puts it thusly: "The test of any economic program or system then is what it does for and to men, women, and children. The human person is worth more than all things material."[21]

Consequently, we propose that free market capitalism allows for the most realistic way to live in the tension between individual dignity and dependence on God. We advocate for the biblical revelation that no one can serve both God and money. We also agree that Christians are called upon to be quite liberal in their giving. Being a steward of God's resources is therefore much more important than either acquiring resources for our gain or letting go of all resources to state control. Such also applies to issues of property. The dignity of the individual is highlighted and supported through ownership of property. Yet, the individual with property has responsibility for taking care of his/her materials as if God is the true property owner. We could accordingly ask, "How can the property, therefore, be used for the love of God and neighbor?"

But how can we afford property if we are not given a fair wage? Christian Realists find in rooted in the principles of Scripture a theme of what is commonly called "equality of opportunity." In other words, everyone should be given the opportunity to start from the same line. How far they run, however, is up to them. There should be equality insured for one to develop and utilize his or her abilities to the best they can.[22] In fact, rather than diminish the dignity of a physically and mentally competent individual by letting them live off the work of others, wages should both accentuate a worker's abilities and complement the quality of life which one's work produces.

Accordingly, for a wage to be considered fair or just in a realistic sense, it should be considered from the standpoint of equity, a most misunderstood word in our contemporary times. In fact, an equitable wage is fairer and more just than an equal wage. Why?

21. Maston, *World Issues*, 120.

22. Maston, *World Issues*, 140–41.

Because equity is required so that equality can come about. Equity, in this sense, refers to a quantitative state of being rather than a qualitative state. A fair wage is one that ensures people get to start from the same line but not necessarily finish at the same line. In practical terms, perhaps we should think more about how to reform the American graduated income tax system or finds ways to give poorer people more purchasing power.[23]

Speaking of being pragmatic, let's get even in further into a more applicable way for Christian Realists to balance the dignity of the individual with the presence of sin in our lives. We are talking here about how Christian Realists can live out their faith in the political arena, granted that we opt for democratic capitalism as more biblically realistic relative to Marxist communism. Thus, it is helpful for us to offer some sound political doctrines for consideration as well as discussing short term strategies to implement such doctrines.

Pragmatic Political Doctrines of Christian Realism

We find six foundational political doctrines of Christian Realism.

First, a new emphasis on the separation of church and state is especially warranted today. Church and state ought to remain separate but highly conversational.

Second, economics and legislation cannot curtail the more generalized problems in the United States. The problem of equal distribution of physical and cultural goods may be the most unsolvable problem given that Americans generally place greater limits on what we grant to others compared to what we grant ourselves in terms of possessions. Also, the interests of the privileged groups (Republicans or Democrats) will be dictated mostly by the lusts of the group's leadership. Accordingly, even socialism or communism will never be fully divorced from special interests, thereby making these theories unfit for doing justice in our society when compared to free market capitalism. A government or political party cannot and should not promise the American people the hope of economic

---

23. Maston, *World Issues*, 142.

and/or social nirvana. Said party can only promise that which is experienced in reality.

Third, the role of government today ought to revert to the intention of the founding fathers, namely to get the government out of the way of the people as much as possible. Government is to be our servant, not our master.

Fourth, there is a way to govern in America through service of others rather than through coerciveness and/or divisiveness. Any valuable compromise between ruling political parties must therefore be judged on two criteria: One, that we must ask if the compromise provide for the exploitation of others, and second, we must ask if the compromise accounts for human limitations, such as the ones that develop and manifest themselves in collective, or tribal, behavior. In other words, is the political compromise actually good for people, or am I simply carrying out the dictates of my peers? Thus, the fundamental value of government is not to force or coerce others to do good as the political party in power sees "good." It is to treat our neighbors as people as persons of value.

Fifth, persuasion is always preferable to coercion. The media oftentimes gives special advantages to a limited amount of views from advertisers and politicians, and that is coercion. However, we must take into account that many Americans desire for their minds to made up for them on important issues affecting the health of the nation. This is dangerous.

We can never quite be sure that we are 100% right and good in our views, so why coerce/impose our "righteousness" on someone else without letting them decide for themselves?

Sixth, collective power must be met with tension/conflict in order to be dislodged. Now is the right time in America for us to decide what in our nation is worth preserving and what must be discarded. These conversations and decisions however will take finesse, persuasion, and compromise.

Pragmatic Political Action for Christian Realists: The Twenty-Five Theses

When Christian Realists consider the foundational principles and doctrines of a sensical proposal for political discourse, some specific, applicable actions emerge. To those ends, we propose twenty-five theses, or disciplines concerning ways one can live out The Balanced Approach in front of his/her neighbors in a way which may stem the tide of either liberal humanism or fundamentalistic legalism. Some disciplines may seem simple and easier to understand than others, but we will give some elaboration to those points which seem more complex in nature.

1. Some people cannot and will not change their minds about trusting in God rather than in themselves. We have found in trying to persuade some people on the Left and Right to take a more balanced approach that some people obstinately cling to their belief systems. It is preferable for balanced Christians to "shake the dust off their feet" when faced with an unwelcoming person or group. Some Christians are so given over to the world's systems that they would rather die defending their system than attempting to discover the kingdom of God. This is their choice, and balanced Christians advocate no kind of coercive behavior or vengeance to sway a person to "our side." The Kingdom of God is not a side to be on but a lifestyle to be lived out.

2. Be critical, prayerful, and theologically reflective about everything. For instance, the realistic Christian will watch the narratives behind the news rather than watch the news itself.

3. Ask ultimate questions. For instance, in the recent turmoil in our nation surrounding the tearing down of statues, the balanced Christian does not argue about the validity of removing statues. He or she asks about and considers those powers and forces that drive the debate in the first place. Christian Realism is not issue-driven but Kingdom-focused.

4. Offer other people an invitation to live in the tension between what is and what ought to be. We are constantly reevaluating

our theology in life of biblical truth. We believe that old credos which have been disproved offer us little in the way of help in becoming more effective as Followers of the Way.

5. Illustrate that both agape love and selfish love are intricately interwoven into our lives. We find, along with the apostle Paul, that at our best as Christians, we still do things that we don't want to do. Power and lust still operate in our flesh even though Jesus put such things to death in us. Put on therefore as little pretense as possible. No one's ideas and intentions are totally pure. The ideas of the progressive left and the conservative right, since they are man-made and a part of the world's systems, can never be divorced from inherent fallenness.

6. Attempt to maintain a healthy sense of humor. We ought to cultivate a desire to laugh at ourselves and not to take life as seriously as some who are hell-bent on maintaining a worldly system of government or administration. We find that the lust for money, sex, and power is incumbent in any world system, and we are all in need of grace. A healthy sense of humor illustrates that we are aiming at serenity in this life, not trying simply to be happy.

7. View with skepticism those who would proclaim their ideas as a "new way" or new approach to vexing human problems. We believe that there is nothing new under the sun on the earth. The "new ways" purported by advocates are simply attempts at self-glorification.

8. View "virtue signaling" with skepticism. Virtue signaling is the action we take in order to show others in power that we fit in or ascribe to their doctrines and dogmas. The virtuous life is that which fulfills the commands of Jesus Christ. We therefore become virtuous when we follow Jesus and deny our own will.

9. Refrain from viewing conflicts between individuals and groups as simple issues of black/white or right/wrong. Conflicts generally arise because people desire to protect their power or economic interests. Conflicts also provide occasions through which people can try to manipulate or exploit their

enemy. A balanced approach desires to find points of compromise among people in conflict rather than coercion.

10. Propose that economic security is not a plausible solution to our problems in life. We recognize money as the root of all evil. Political interests as ultimately wrapped up in economic interests. The tension between socialists on the theological and political left and the capitalists of the theological and religious right likely will never be solved.

11. Look with skepticism upon the views of those who justify their actions as benefitting the common good.

12. Offer a peaceful way to live in tension between the left and right while avoiding political coercion. We simply should not view things through the one-sided lenses of "justice" or "conservatism." In fact, the labels we use for classifying another's belief systems often fall greatly short of God's glory and contribute to an unwinnable word game in our culture. Balanced Christians have little desire to play word games.

13. Pray for our enemies rather than destroying them. Grieve when we see those things which are worth preserving in our culture annihilated in the name of purging evil.

14. Advocate for repentance. True salvation is by God's grace through faith in Jesus Christ.

15. Commend that life is not fulfilling without the mercy of God.

16. View every problem in our culture as theological in nature. Thus, the kingdom of God has relevancy in every aspect of human life.

17. Help churches to recognize how and why they have turned in on themselves and have, for the present time, rejected the Kingdom of God.

18. Offer a way of living in relationship with others, especially with those whom we are in conflict. Accordingly, rejects domination and isolation of enemies. In fact, it is even advantageous to reject "tolerance" as it is defined in contemporary culture. To simply tolerate someone else avoids relationship building and is contrary to the way of the Kingdom.

19. Question our quest for happiness, as such is defined by our culture.

20. Offer solutions to life's problems in a more qualitative way. Life is not to be reduced to numbers and statistics.
21. Equate pretension with idealism. There are always limits on our knowledge.
22. Group dynamics can greatly affect and individual's behavior and attitude. Be aware that peer pressure is not outdated.
23. Offer an effective approach for raising power against another power. We do not advocate accommodation but compromise. Any compromise between powers, however, must take into account our human capacity for exploitation of others.
24. Recognize that much of the arguing between the left and right today boils down to the equal distribution of goods and wealth. Both sides are interested in what is "fair." The balanced approach suggests that the problem of inequity may never be solved, but there are steps that Christians can take to mitigate disaster among our neighbors. For instance, since we believe that economic interests are at the core of the conflict between the right and left, we see how both groups display imperialistic ambitions. The special interests of elitists remain important within the leadership structures and systems of both groups. Thus, the ones with lesser power in the group are always put in the vulnerable position of being willing victims of those in power, and they are stoked on by a utopian (and thus impossible) ideal. As the kingdom of God comes on earth as it is in heaven, it is conceivable that a community can prevent unequal rewards being put into the systems of social power.
25. Offer ways for skeptics to avoid defeatism.

A Closing Confession and Commitment

We confess that *what is* seems to matter inherently more than what is to be. Yet, Christian Realism, at its core, has a commitment to the impossible possibility of seeing God's kingdom come and will be done to complete fruition on earth as it is in heaven. The greatest reality is a fully reconciled relationship between God and the individual. In the meantime, those of us of the Christian Realism persuasion may apply the Balanced Approach, striving to walk as Jesus walked (1 John 2:6).

We accordingly seek not to divide and conquer through either the legalism of the Right or the idealistic humanism of the Left. We find it best to take up our crosses by living in the tension of both the now and the eschaton. We view the unsolvable dilemmas of our day with both furrowed brows and the hint of a grin, knowing that we see through a glass darkly now, and we do not have the infinite mind or strength to provide any sort of one-size-fits-all program for human peace and prosperity. Yet, we walk by the Spirit, courageously pressing on to the prize God has promised us.

Will you therefore join a movement in which we resolutely stand for the greatest good of loving God and loving neighbor while not trying to make a crow into a fence? You are invited and welcome at the table of consecrated common sense.

Bibliography

Bennett, John C. *Christian Realism*. New York: Scribner, 1941.

Berger, Peter. *The Sacred Canopy*. New York: Anchor, 1969.

Brunner, Emil. *The Divine Imperative*. Philadelphia: Westminster, 1979.

Coffin, William Sloane. "Liberty to the Captives and Good Tidings to the Afflicted." In *Homosexuality and Christian Faith: Questions of Conscience for the Churches*, edited by Walter Wink, 105–10. Minneapolis, MN: Fortress, 1999.

Diefenthaler, John. *The Paradox of Church and World: Selected Writings of H. Richard Niebuhr*. Minneapolis: Fortress, 2015.

Maston, T. B. *Christianity and World Issues*. New York: Macmillan, 1965.

Mosteller, Timothy. *The Heresy of Heresies: A Defense of Common-Sense Realism*. Eugene, OR: Cascade, 2021.

Newbigin, Lesslie. *The Gospel in a Pluralist Society*. Grand Rapids: Eerdmans, 1989.

Niebuhr, H. Richard. *Radical Monotheism and Western Culture*. Louisville: Westminster John Knox, 1993.

———. *The Kingdom of God in America*. Middletown, CT: Wesleyan University Press, 1988.

———. *The Responsible Self: An Essay in Christian Moral Philosophy*. New York: Harper & Row, 1963.

Niebuhr, Reinhold. *The Children of Light and The Children of Darkness: A Vindication of Democracy and a Critique of Its Traditional Defense*. Chicago: The University of Chicago Press, 2011.

———. *The Essential Reinhold Niebuhr*. New Haven: Yale University Press, 1986.

——— *The Nature and Destiny of Man*. Louisville: Westminster John Knox, 1996.

Tillich, Paul. *Dynamics of Faith*. New York: Harper, 1957.

———. *The Essential Tillich*. Edited by F. Forrester Church. Chicago: The University of Chicago Press, 1987.

www.ingramcontent.com/pod-product-compliance
Lightning Source LLC
Chambersburg PA
CBHW071948100426
42736CB00042B/2414